CONTENTS

GETTING STARTED

> "If kids struggle to do what needs to get done to accomplish their goals, they are going to struggle with a lot of things in life. It's important to understand executive function so we can give kids what they need to build a successful future— and also give them a good quality of life now."

— SETH PERLER

Walking into a room of 27, 28, or even 30 students is overwhelming. Especially when you consider their varying skills, abilities, learning styles, and behavior. That's how I felt as a first-year teacher, anyway.

I remember my first day so vividly - I was excited to finally be able to make a difference in children's lives but apprehensive because I was unsure what my class would be like and, to be frank, my own capabilities.

It's worth bearing in mind that this was 20-odd years ago, and the support for students in educational settings wasn't what it is today. Take neurodiversity. Neurodiversity is the acknowledgment that everyone's brain differs; we all experience the world and interact with it differently.

When I started teaching, neurodiversity wasn't well-recognized in education (or elsewhere!). Thankfully, there have been many improvements in the last two decades. But even today, we have to be very careful with the language we use when describing neurodiverse people because so many terms insinuate inferiority or otherness, like 'disability' and 'deficit.' I'll explain my first day to give you an idea of what it was like back then.

My first day is seared into my brain - it's not a day I'll ever forget. Three children, in particular, were extremely challenging. One student was a foster child who had suffered some horrible traumas. Another presented with what would now be diagnosed as Oppositional Defiance Disorder (ODD). The third had hearing difficulties. And that's not even mentioning the students whose middle name was impulsivity, where self-control was nowhere to be seen. Then, there were the daydreamers, who would be happy to just stare out the window all day rather than entertain the thought of starting work on their own. Of course, I couldn't get any of them to answer a single question.

I had spent my years of training and previous weeks in preparation, ensuring I knew all of the theory inside out. However, as soon as I stepped foot in the classroom and began to teach, I quickly realized that I could try to teach the curriculum until I was blue in the face. Yet, if my class can't concentrate, behave, or are struggling in other ways neurologically, they won't be able to take in what I'm teaching them.

That's the thing about being a teacher. We spend so much of our time trying to get our students to focus, manage their own time, and organize themselves that there's little time left in the day to actually teach. How are you supposed to get it all done?

From my 23 years of experience, I have found that many students struggle with fundamental brain skills, like working memory, flexible thinking, self-control, task initiation, and self-reflection. How can we expect them to take in a full curriculum if they struggle with these essential competencies?

Many teachers know this - I'm sure this isn't new to you. Yet, due to the constant strain we're under from lack of support in the classroom, the time it takes for a child to receive a diagnosis and get the help they need, plus the enormous time pressure we're under to deliver the curriculum and see progression in grades, it can seem like an enormous task to do anything more than what's required of us - teach the curriculum. I don't know about you, but this has often left me feeling like I'm not doing enough for my students; that I'm letting them down.

That's where this book can help. Over my time as an educator, I have accumulated the knowledge I present to you in this book. I stress that this is all I have learned *so far* - I continue to enrich my understanding every day I spend in a school with every unique child I meet.

I have spent many hours working closely with psychologists to generate the best plan of action for students with executive deficits based on formal assessments of executive functioning.

For the past 7 years, I have worked closely with students with executive function challenges, providing support within student services. What's more, I'm a mom to two teenagers, one of whom is neurodiverse. My experience as an educator and mom and my passion for seeing success in the classroom is the driving force behind this book.

I've seen firsthand how the strategies contained within can help students on a daily basis and ease the pressure on teachers like yourself who are trying to individualize their teaching to a neurodiverse classroom. With these tools, you can spend less time in stress mode and more time enjoying your class and the wonderful students within it.

IS THIS BOOK RIGHT FOR ME?

For teachers, time is precious; I understand this more than most. You want to be confident you're spending your time wisely. That may lead you to the question: is this book right for me? To answer that, let's paint a picture of what this book can provide.

Envision this. You begin the day with a short executive functioning exercise that your students find fun and engaging. They're immediately more focused than when they came into class. You start your first lesson - this time, you don't have children looking longingly out the window or talking over you. There's no one misbehaving every time you turn away. All of your students are engaged and ready to learn.

You start sprinkling short games and exercises into your teaching that help to strengthen your student's executive functioning skills. Quickly, you start hitting your teaching goals. You see progression in your student's grades. But the frosting on the cake - your students are happy, enthusiastic, and eagerly listen in while you teach.

This scenario may seem out of reach now, but when you break down the barriers of executive functioning, it's not long until this dream becomes a reality.

To begin with, I thought it would be super hard to bring in executive function activities. I visualized the students not showing the slightest interest, and it taking up a massive portion of my day just to get through. I was shocked that it wasn't like this at all. The problem I found is that it's not in the curriculum to teach our students how to learn. We teach them what they should be learning, but we don't teach them how to take in that information, process it, and keep it in their heads. They need this skill if they're going to do well in the classroom.

That's why I feel it's important to share it here with you. If I can help you introduce executive functioning skills into your classroom in a simple, straightforward way that's fun for you and your students, that's a win for me.

WHAT WILL I GET OUT OF THIS BOOK?

"Is this book right for me?" may quickly be followed by "what am I going to get out of this book?" This book is packed with information on executive function, collected over two decades of working with children who struggle with these skills. Peppered through this book are real-life, relatable examples that I'm sure many of us have come across during our time as educators or parents - I know I have!

I've given you a short self assessment sheet to support this knowledge at the end of the book. You can use the QR code provided for easier copying purposes. Give your kids these to fill out to help you better understand where they're struggling, EF-wise.

Within, you'll also find loads of fun, easy activities that will help your students build on their executive function skills. In my experience, the students end up really enjoying these and sometimes even ask if we can do them again! There are also worksheets and helpful visuals that you can print off and use in class. These are yours to adapt, annotate, or edit as much as you want - do whatever suits the children you work with and your teaching style!

Finally, this book is to remind you you're not on your own. Teaching is hard, especially when your students have complex needs. Just by reading this book, you're doing the best you can with the tools that you have. By the time we're through, you'll have more tools in your toolkit to support your students.

Shall we get started?

THE 411 ON EXECUTIVE FUNCTION

Think about your adult brain for a second. Are there times when you find it difficult to focus? Have you recently been in a situation where it was challenging to regulate your emotions? And was there ever a time when you struggled to remember instructions, even though they were made super clear? If we adults were school students, we'd probably all have our hands up right now.

Skills like concentrating, regulating emotions, and multitasking are tricky to master, even for adults who aren't neurodiverse. Can we honestly expect children to be good at these?

In this chapter, I give you the 411 on executive function (EF), including the three main areas involved, the seven EF skills, and the importance of executive function for healthy development. We'll also delve into how neurotypical, neurodiverse, and 2e children typically differ in executive function.

This chapter is jam-packed with stories and personal anecdotes so you can see the impact learning about these skills and strategies had on my life, and the time I spent in the classroom.

WHAT IS EXECUTIVE FUNCTION?

The term "executive function" sounds way too complicated for my liking. So, let's break it down. Executive function is a group of brain skills we use daily - they help us focus, adapt to change, handle difficult emotions, and manage our impulses.

In essence, this group of skills acts as a management center in our brain. Without them, we may find it challenging to do what other people consider 'simple' tasks like setting goals, planning how we will achieve them, and the process of attaining them.

When it comes to EF, there are three main areas:

1. **Working memory:** the ability to hold information in mind temporarily or while we need it. We need working memory whenever a task requires more than just memorization.
2. **Cognitive flexibility (or 'flexible thinking'):** being able to change your thinking and behavior in

response to changes in your environment, including adjusting to evolving rules and thinking about multiple things simultaneously.

3. **Inhibitory control (including self-control):** stopping yourself from acting on impulses - automatic responses - using attention and reasoning. This skill helps you to prevent behaving inappropriately in situations that require a more thought-out response.

Children who struggle with these skills are likely to face challenges in all areas of life, including school, home, and, later on, at work.

But let's be clear. Clinically undiagnosed EF isn't a learning disability - you can have any level of intelligence and still have executive functioning difficulty. Improving EF skills is just like anything else. With most of them, it just takes practice. The brain is a muscle; like hitting the gym, your brain needs a workout to grow and develop.

WHY IS EXECUTIVE FUNCTION SO IMPORTANT?

It's easier to describe the importance of executive function using imagery. So, here goes. Let's compare a student's brain to an air traffic control tower at an airport. If this airport is busy, many planes will land and take off. All of these times must be coordinated to ensure there aren't any horrible crashes.

Just like air traffic control prevents plane crashes, executive function stops many of brain skills from crashing, including:

- Organization
- Planning
- Information processing

With executive function, we can manage incoming information, attend to that and our surroundings, plan things in advance, and stick to rules and regulations. Executive function also stops an overload of information that can overwhelm us and cause dysregulation.

Without air traffic control, things will likely fall apart quickly. Not only will there be a general lack of organization, but also, the people trying to land the planes will feel stressed, under pressure, and confused. That's how it can feel for young people with EF difficulties.

What's more, without EF, people will struggle to learn. These skills are the building blocks of learning. But, as I said earlier, we can often build upon (or compensate for) our EF skills. Many people, teachers included, believe that once you're born with EF difficulties, you're stuck with them for life; you can't grow and develop. While it may not be possible to actually change all of our EF capabilities, we can undoubtedly use strategies and accommodations to compensate for these so that we can engage in learning.

You may be asking, "where's the evidence?" Well, research by Diamond and colleagues (2007) found that EF skills are vital for school and life success. In their study, EF skills correlate with school readiness and academic achievement (including math and reading) from preschool to high school.

Their research found that many children lack EF skills when they first start school, and, unfortunately for us, teachers aren't explicitly told how to teach EF (although everything we do - schedules, lists, planning, transitions - does support EF). However, they discovered that children as young as 4 and 5 show improvements in EF when regular educators incorporate EF activities into their teaching. And the more an activity needs EF skills, the more significant the academic advancement.

And the improvements don't end there. When we begin to work on EF, not only will we see positive changes in brain skills and school success, but we'll also see improvements in mental health. This may be the most significant change of all for our young students.

As educators, we need to be able to spot EF difficulties in our students so we can provide support. Let's take a look at the common signs.

SIGNS A STUDENT IS STRUGGLING WITH EF

Problems with EF can often manifest similarly to signs of ADHD - the two look alike in some ways. Why is this? Simply, ADHD involves difficulties in EF.

Here are some common signs that a student is struggling with EF skills:

- They find it tricky to start or complete a task without 1-1 help
- They're unsure how to order tasks in terms of importance
- They quickly forget information they have read or heard
- They have difficulty following tasks that have a series of steps
- They're unsure how to manage their time effectively
- They become anxious or display challenging behaviors in response to changes in their regular routine
- They display difficulty focusing on one task after finishing another
- They frequently forget where they have put their belongings

While anyone can have EF difficulties, this is more common amongst neurodiverse individuals, such as those with ADHD or autism.

So, what are the main EF skills? And how do they affect learning?

THE 7 EXECUTIVE FUNCTION SKILLS

There are 7 main executive function skills:

1. Planning, organizing, and time management
2. Working memory
3. Flexible thinking
4. Task initiation
5. Attention/focus
6. Perseverance
7. Self-reflection

Let's explore each of these in turn.

Planning, Organizing, and Time Management

We all know what the morning rush is like. If you have a child with EF difficulties, you know this better than most. Perhaps there have been multiple occasions where you have told your child to get dressed and brush their teeth while you rush off to sort another task, only for you to return 10 minutes later to see they haven't budged. This is an example of a child struggling with planning and organizing their time.

Sometimes, giving verbal instructions on their own just doesn't work for children with EF difficulties. Instead, combine your verbal prompts with a visual, like a simple egg timer, when it's time for them to clean their teeth and get dressed. This reduces the stress felt by yourself and your child in the early hours of the day and sets the right tone for a better day ahead.

Working Memory

Forgetting why you've just gone into a room is an example of a working memory error that I like to offer people whenever they're unsure what working memory is. Another common one is forgetting what you were saying mid-sentence.

In terms of children in a school setting, a student with working memory difficulties may find it challenging to solve a complex math question with several stages of working out. They might also be unable to keep in mind any verbal directions you give them. In this scenario, it can help to offer visual prompts or to provide an outline of the main points you are trying to get across to them.

Flexible Thinking

Imagine that your pen ran out of ink right in the middle of writing something important. What would you do? If you have strong, flexible thinking skills, you'd probably get up and grab another pen or ask someone for one.

But this situation could play out a lot differently for people who have difficulties with flexible thinking. If a student with flexible thinking problems was sitting for an exam and their pen stopped working, they may think, "I have no pen to write, so I can't finish my assignment." They may then sit the rest of the exam silently, not writing a word.

Rigid thinking means only seeing a single solution to a problem. If that one solution doesn't work, a rigid thinker may struggle to come up with any alternative actions. You can see how this can be massively problematic!

Task Initiation

Task initiation is all about getting started. It's the ability to start a task at the best time without procrastinating beforehand.

An example of this that's common among students is starting an assignment. While some kids will start it immediately, others procrastinate until the last few hours before the paper is due, then quickly scribble down their essays or scribble a quick answer before the recess bell rings.

It's important to remember that task initiation requires independence - if a child needs lots of support to get started on a task, they likely struggle with it.

Attention/Focus

Attention involves concentrating on what you have to do. You've probably seen many students struggle with this. Attention also includes being able to focus on what you're doing, even when there are distractions around.

A typical example of attention difficulties is daydreaming. Have you ever noticed one of your students get side-tracked by tiny distractions, like a fly traveling across the room or another child tapping their pencil?

Perhaps you've witnessed a student that becomes frustrated when there is any background noise while trying to complete their work, even if it's you trying to help another student. These scenarios are so common in children who have attention problems.

Perseverance

Perseverance is an amazing skill to master. Take JK Rowling - if she hadn't tried again after Harry Potter had been rejected by 12 different publishers, we wouldn't know the magical world of Harry, Ron, and Hermoine.

For students, perseverance is continuing to work towards your goals even when you come up against challenges. This could be standing up in front of the class and giving a presentation. The student may be dreading it, worried sick about embarrassing themselves in front of their classmates. Perseverance would be working hard at preparing by studying. A child who struggles with determination may call in sick or procrastinate.

Self-Reflection

Without self-reflection, all of us will struggle to grow and develop. For students, self-reflection may be reading or hearing the feedback from teachers - rather than just looking at their grades - to ensure they do better next time

A student who has self-reflection difficulties may continue to make the same mistakes repeatedly and struggle to identify how they're feeling, what they're thinking, and the consequences of their actions.

Self-reflection also involves identifying your strengths. It's important to know what you're good at!

HOW EF HELPS NEURODIVERSE STUDENTS

Before we unpick how EF helps neurodiverse students, we need to identify the difference between three key terms:

1. Neurotypical
2. Neurodiverse
3. 2e

A "neurotypical" child would be one whose way of thinking, perceiving, and behaving in the world is considered to fit into the "norm" of what's expected in the general population. Of course, there's no such thing as "normal," but we'd need a-whole-nother book for that!

Neurodiversity is considered neuroatypical - it refers to children who see the world differently and think in a different way to what is believed to be the "norm" among the general population. They may also act in alternative ways. This term is most often used to describe those on the autism spectrum and people with ADHD, dyslexia, Down syndrome, dyspraxia, dyscalculia, dysgraphia, and so on.

2e stands for twice exceptional, and it's called this because these people are believed to have two "exceptionalities" - giftedness and learning disabilities. Around 5% of kids are 2e.

Twice-exceptional students tend to be creative, quirky, very intelligent, and experience deep emotions - they have super cool brains and think very differently from the rest of us. This means that the potential impact they could make on the world is massive if their educational needs are met and the people around them support them in the way they need.

Their talents may be:

- Problem-solving
- IQ
- Intuition
- Abstract thinking
- Academic
- Creativity
- Artistry
- Visual-spatial
- Kinesthetic

And so on. Potential learning difficulties among 2e kids could be:

- Speech & language
- Aspergers
- ADHD
- Autism
- Dyslexia
- Emotional disorders
- Processing disorders

2e children tend to develop very asynchronously. What I mean by this is that they may be a seventh grader who can solve math questions at college level, read at fourth-grade level and write at tenth-grade level. They may be able to converse very well with adults about particular topics but appear emotionally immature when it comes to doing tasks they don't enjoy.

Unfortunately, many 2e children can't reach their full potential because they're not given the proper support. One reason for this is executive function - it's not uncommon for 2e children to struggle with EF skills. And because building on EF skills isn't part of the school curriculum, it becomes easier for these exceptional students to fall through the cracks.

Then, there are 3e students. These children fall into the 2e category *and* are part of a marginalized community. In this sense, they're thrice exceptional, with the third exceptionality being cultural. Teachers like us need to make accommodations for these students to support their exceptionalities - Dr. Russell Barkely describes this need as similar to a physical disability requiring a wheelchair; it helps the children get where they need to go.

2e and 3e students generally struggle with different EF skills, depending on their exact learning difficulties. For example, children with ADHD tend to find inhibitory control particularly hard. They typically act impulsively without thinking their behaviors through. They also often struggle with self-monitoring their work, leading to errors. ADHD also frequently goes hand-in-hand with working memory problems. Delaying immediate gratification may be especially hard for these kids, particularly those that find time management tricky.

Whereas children with ASD tend to struggle more with flexible thinking. They may get stuck on an idea or a single solution to a problem, not seeing all other potential options. Because of this, they may find it difficult to transition between tasks, adapt to change, and solve problems. Poor emotional control is also common in those with ASD.

It's important to remember that no child is the same - even if you have two children with ADHD in your class, they will probably struggle with different areas of executive functioning. Therefore, when teaching EF, there's no one-size-fits-all.

Teaching EF in schools (and, for parents, in the home!) can help children to build on these skills so they don't experience the same challenges when it comes to learning. So, how can parents teach EF at home?

HOW TO START TEACHING EF IN THE HOME

As EF isn't part of the curriculum, teaching these skills has previously fallen on parents' shoulders. Some parents have tried this, while others have hired EF "coaches" to teach them how to incorporate EF skill-building activities into their everyday lives.

EF skills should be taught regularly over an extended period; I recommend at least a few months. Children struggling with EF also need a growth environment where they can develop skills through play and social interactions.

It helps incorporate routines and structure and build solid and reliable relationships, making the world feel more predictable and safer for these children. You can help your child gain independence in their routine through visuals like a visual timetable, now and next board, and lists or by putting away distractions.

In terms of building relationships, find activities your child likes to do and do them together. Having common interests allows you to have fun together, create relationship rituals, and better understand each other's personalities. Children with positive relationships with their parents are more likely to develop strong relationships with others, so it's well worth your time.

According to The Parent Practice, 80% of parenting is modeling (Clark, 2022). As parents, modeling healthy behaviors helps our children to understand how we solve problems, use logic to come up with solutions, and regulate our emotions.

Part of providing a safe growth environment is to give them independence. Let them try out skills like problem-solving and emotion regulation in the home environment; you won't always be at hand to offer solutions and guidance. Of course, if they want it, offer it. Giving them space for growth will help them gain confidence, so they can use these skills independently in school and work environments.

WHAT'S NEXT?

In this chapter, we've discussed the different executive function skills and their importance for everyday life and learning. Naturally, the brain plays a huge role in all of these functions. So, in the following chapter, we'll dive into the science of EF with a bit of background on the human brain to help our understanding of how it ties in with EF.

But first, on the following few pages, you'll find an interactive exercise containing a brief summary of all the EF skills and a chart on EF development by age. This is for you to print off, work through, or adapt as you like. Enjoy!

Interactive Exercise

PLANNING: Coming up with a strategy before you start a task.

Strategies for teachers to use with students:

1. *Personalized timetables - allow your students to color-code these and label the lessons. Print out lots of copies, as some students may also need them for their desks and lockers!*
2. *Use a daily schedule so students can see you modeling planning skills.*
3. *Play games that rely on planning ahead, like chess.*
4. *Begin each day by going through the daily targets - what do you expect your students to get out of the day? For younger children (around Grade 2), you could use "wishes" instead of "goals" or explain that these are the things that will make them "star learners."*

ORGANIZATION: Following a system to keep your belongings in order and keep track of your plans.

Strategies for teachers to use with students:

1. *Give students a calendar or planner. Not all kids will know how to use these, so go through it with them first!*
2. *Incorporate tidying away into your end-of-lesson time. Model appropriate tidying away for students who don't know how to do this. This could involve clearing your desk*

or a communal table, putting everything away in the correct location, and preparing it for the next day!

3. *At the beginning & end of the day, allow your students time to organize their materials.*
4. *Dish out classroom jobs to each student. Place a 'job chart' on display so they can keep track of when it's their turn. Include desk/cubby checks in this chart to help promote self-organization.*

TIME-MANAGEMENT: Making the most of your time to complete tasks effectively.

Strategies for teachers to use with students:

1. *At the beginning of the year, create big SMART goals and lots of smaller goals and make these visible. This will help your students stay focused.*
2. *Play a game where people talk as quickly as they can for 30 seconds, then speak at a slow pace. Discuss as a group the importance of pacing yourself.*
3. *Allow your students to create their own visual timetable.*
4. *Encourage your students to create a priorities list.*

WORKING MEMORY: Keeping information in mind while you need it.

Strategies for teachers to use with students:

1. *Add brain games into your lessons, like sudoku & chess.*

2. *Play memory games like "Concentration" or who can say the alphabet backward the quickest.*
3. *Give card games like Go Fish, Uno, and Crazy Eights a go.*
4. *Make your lessons multi-sensory by including elements of taste, touch, hearing, or smell.*

FLEXIBLE THINKING: Adapt your ideas and strategies when things change.

Strategies for teachers to use with students:

1. *Use optical illusions like the 'elephant legs' or 'Kanizsa triangle' to discuss seeing things from different perspectives.*
2. *Practice stress-relieving exercises such as mindfulness and deep breathing to encourage self-regulation.*
3. *Adapt popular strategy and logic games like Chutes and Ladders - use activities that require your students to use word-play and puns.*

TASK INITIATION: Starting tasks independently.

Strategies for teachers to use with students:

1. *Give your students a 'movement break' before starting lessons. This could involve heavy movements like push ups, or it could be more calming movements. Movement breaks will help them get rid of extra*

energy, and they'll learn that it's time to learn once this is over.

2. *Teach your students to take 'brain breaks' when transitioning between tasks or use them as a reward for achieving a working goal.*
3. *Use a timer to show them how long you expect them to work on a particular task.*
4. *Provide step-by-step visuals with directions breaking down how to get started.*

ATTENTION/FOCUS: Focusing on one task for a period of time.

Strategies for teachers to use with students:

1. *Play Simon Says when your students are getting distracted.*
2. *Keep your classroom clutter-free and your display boards simple so your students won't get distracted by them.*
3. *Break up tasks into more manageable chunks, and teach your students to do the same.*
4. *Play Red-Light-Green-Light to help your students improve their concentration skills.*

PERSEVERANCE: Staying on-task and not giving up even when it gets tricky.

Strategies for teachers to use with students:

1. *Don't rush in to save your students; let them struggle a little bit. This can help teach perseverance.*
2. *Have an egg and spoon race or ring toss game.*
3. *Teach your students about role models who persevered, like J. K. Rowling, Michael Jordan, and Walt Disney.*
4. *Make a list of positive self-talk, like "I am trying my best" and "I can do this."*

SELF-REFLECTION: Thinking about your learning and what you can do to grow and develop.

Strategies for teachers to use with students:

1. *Work through feedback as a whole class.*
2. *Make time for work re-dos.*
3. *Encourage your students to look at essay feedback and set themselves three goals for their next assignment.*
4. *Assign reflection buddies so your students can think about their work with a partner.*
5. *Create a "Bump it Up" wall. Bump-it-up walls are a form of self-assessment that help students to see their learning progress. When their progress is clear and visible, and they can see the goal they're working towards, this naturally motivates them to work hard.*

EF SKILL DEVELOPMENT ACCORDING TO AGE

	INFANT 0 - 24 months	TODDLER 2 - 4 years	EARLY LEARNER 5 - 12 years	TEEN 13 - 16 years	YOUNG ADULT 18+
Planning	Pointing, grabbing, and focusing on objects.	Can complete simple tasks and follow straightforward instructions.	Can follow a series of steps to achieve an end-goal. Able to play games requiring tactics and strategy.	Can plan out a sequence of steps needed to complete a task like an assignment. Regularly planning social occasions and organize group work.	Can work towards multiple goals, making more than one plan at a given time. Can identify and meet long-term goals.
Organization	Colors, size, and shape are interesting. Begin to be able to match.	Beginning to gain an idea of how things fall into categories and patterns. Can tidy away belongings with support.	Able to follow simple checklists. Can now organize and sequence more complex stories.	Handles both school and home routines with ease. Can now utilize resources to help organize homework and assignments.	Can be neat, orderly, and re-organize if needed.
Time Management	NOT YET DEVELOPED	Time concepts like days, weeks, and seasons are starting to make sense. Able to wait for short periods of time.	Starting to estimate time and developing an understanding of task duration. Starting to differentiate required tasks from leisure time and organize time accordingly.	Can give accurate estimations of the duration of tasks and changes working speed in accordance. Actively attempts to avoid the consequences of bad time-management.	Able to use tools to manage their time more effectively. Starts to adjust timetables to meet changing time requirements.

Working Memory	Show enjoyment at known rhymes and rhythms. Can participate in simple recall games.	Able to follow the movements and steps in fingerplays and can follow a tune.	Can play with puzzles and simple games independently. Ability to collect information and transfer this knowledge to different settings is improving.	Independence when playing games and activities, including group exercises. Can collect and apply information to a variety of environments.	Uses multiple sources of information to meet long-term goals. This period marks the best working memory capacity.
Flexible Thinking	Towards the end of this age range, children begin to play straightforward role play and imaginative play games.	Starting to switch between activities. Will handle sudden changes to routine and transitions without dysregulati- on on some occasions.	Able to engage in activities where changes frequently occur, like sports and games, but still requiring some adult support.	May still require some adult support to help come up with strategies to cope with unexpected changes to routine.	Sudden changes to routine can cause some stress, but they are largely able to deal with the unpredictability. Able to modify actions and timetable to meet ever-changing environmental demands.
Task Initiation	NOT YET DEVELOPED	Can start a task independently and complete it if its duration is 10 minutes or under.	Can start and complete 30 - 60 minute tasks.	Can start and complete 60 - 90 minute tasks independently.	Able to manage distractions and unfavorable situations to still get tasks done. Now, planning and prioritizing are a normal pre-task activity.

	INFANT 0 - 24 months	TODDLER 2 - 4 years	EARLY LEARNER 5 - 12 years	TEEN 13 - 16 years	YOUNG ADULT 18+
Attention Focus	Begin to copy and imitate. Can respond to peek-a-boo and pat-a-cake games.	Can direct attention onto activities and objects for longer than previously. Can be redirected by an adult to pay attention.	Starting to develop money saving skills to buy preferred objects. Can use tools like reminders and note-taking to help maintain concentration.	Developing empathy and understanding of the emotions of others. Although unsure how to manage them yet, teens have some experience with 'adult emotions.'	Can manipulate, change and remove distractions on occasions, and can still attend even when distractions are present.
Perseverance	Show determination to have their needs met, capture attention, and reach for objects like toys. Learning new movements like rolling over from their back to their stomach, crawling, and walking.	Trying activities in which they are naturally skilled leads them to attempt those out of their comfort zone where perseverance is key.	Starting to learn more complex motor movements that require perseverance like dressing themselves and drinking out of normal cups.	Able to persevere with various tasks including homework and leisure activities, but may still need some support from adults at times.	Now, confidently able to persevere in tasks that are challenging in order to meet long-term goals.
Self Reflection	NOT YET DEVELOPED	Has some understanding and is able to communicate their own feelings. Can make simple connections between these and behaviours. Can play with other children, either by directing or accepting direction.	Are able to complete self-reflective tasks like journaling independently. Can conduct a simple analysis of their work to identify minor errors.	Can make adjustments and improvements to work based on feedback and self-monitoring. May still need some support from adults to help self-reflection process.	Can self-monitor and check own work, comparing it with others.

THE SCIENCE BEHIND EF AND THE BRAIN

The brain is a weird and wonderful thing. It's made up of multiple parts that communicate using over 100 trillion connections. To understand executive function, we must understand the basics of our brains. Don't worry; I've gone for a straightforward approach in this chapter rather than super sciencey!

Chapter 2 is about how the brain works and develops in children. We'll think about how this affects their emotional reaction to difficult situations and the best way that we, as educators and parents, can respond to little people when they show us their big, big emotions.

THE MECHANISMS OF THE BRAIN

The brain is one of the most important elements of our nervous system. Completing any action would be out of the question without our handy brains. Our brains have four distinct parts:

1. Cerebellum
2. Cerebrum
3. Brain stem
4. Limbic system

Each brain area has roles in which they specialize. The cerebellum is essential for balance, gait, and muscle tone, while the cerebrum's primary functions are planning, problem-solving, reasoning, feelings, and our world perceptions.

The management of blood pressure, heart rate, and respiration is all down to the brain stem, and the limbic system helps to regulate our drives, such as hunger and thirst, as well as emotions, fear, and memories.

The prefrontal cortex is the brain area we're mainly focusing on in this book. This brain region is part of the cerebrum and takes up the whole front third of our brain - it sits right behind your eyes and forehead. The prefrontal cortex plays a role in the EF skills such as planning cognitive behavior, decision-making, controlling our social behavior, and personality expression. Therefore, this brain region has the biggest say when it comes to our personality, values, and goals.

But it does more than this. It's also the control center of our brain - it regulates our thoughts and behaviors so they align with our personal goals. The prefrontal cortex, as a result, supports learning.

The prefrontal cortex is closely related to the amygdala, a kidney bean-sized area in the middle of the brain involved in our stress response. Fundamentally, this brain region detects stress, then sends a message to the hypothalamus telling it to respond. This is what sets off our fight-or-flight response.

The prefrontal cortex's job is to manage our emotional responses once the amygdala detects stress. If the brain areas could talk, the prefrontal cortex would say to the amygdala, "Hey, it's OK. This thing isn't as stressful as you first thought it was." In this way, the prefrontal cortex is crucial in calming our bodies down in non-threatening situations.

HOW THE BRAIN DEVELOPS

Jean Piaget was one of the most influential psychologists and genetic epistemologists of all time, mainly because of his theory on cognitive development. In 1952, Piaget set out to answer questions about how children's brains develop. As a result of his findings, he proposed four distinct stages of brain development:

1. **Sensorimotor Stage (birth - 2 years):** When children learn about their external surroundings through sight, smell, touch, taste, and hearing and by manipulating objects.

2. **Preoperational Stage (2 - 7 years):** When imagination and memory develop, allowing children to understand the symbolism of things and appreciate past and future ideas.

3. **Concrete Operational Stage (7 - 11 years):** Awareness of things happening around them grows, and the understanding of others' perspectives and emotions develops. They become less self-centered and recognize that others' wants and beliefs differ from their own.

4. **Formal Operational Stage (11+):** Begin to use logic during problem-solving, when seeing the world, and planning for the future.

According to this theory, attention and short- and long-term memory doesn't develop until 2 - 5 years, and auditory processing doesn't show up until 5 - 7 years. Auditory perception is an essential skill for reading. 5 years appears to be a fundamental time, as logic and reasoning also develop then.

These four stages help us understand what's going on in children's brains at different points in their lives. It's important to remember that children may struggle with specific tasks, not because they don't want to do them but because the tasks ask for more brain power than their young minds can handle.

One thing to know about the brain in terms of executive function is that it develops "back to front." The areas at the base of the brain, like the brain stem and limbic system, develop first. The prefrontal cortex is the last part of the brain to mature - it doesn't fully develop until age 25. And that's among neurotypical people! According to Dr. Russel Barkely, ADHD can delay executive function development by 30%.

When children face difficult situations beyond their brain development stage, this often results in a display of big emotions. Let's talk more about that next.

HELPING LITTLE PEOPLE WITH THEIR BIG EMOTIONS

Whether you're an educator or a parent, I'm sure you're well aware that children are capable of expressing big emotions. Even if you haven't got direct experience, I'm sure you've heard a toddler's heart-wrenching sob in the mall or grocery store.

Often, children express big emotions when they don't have the tools to handle the current situation - perhaps they don't know how to ask for what they want, or they can't understand why a particular situation is playing out the way it is. Whatever it is, they lack the skills at that moment in time to manage the intensity of their emotions. This is called dysregulation - when the demands in their external environment exceed their capacity to cope in a calm, controlled way.

What does dysregulation look like? It may take the form of:

- Crying
- Slamming doors
- Stomping feet
- Hitting out
- Shouting

All of these are very outward reactions. However, there are also less easily-recognizable signs of dysregulation, like withdrawing and shutting down.

Don't worry; dysregulation is a natural response to threats. It would be a bigger course for concern if our children *weren't* crying when we left them. Becoming upset at a parent's absence is developmentally appropriate and shows they have a strong bond with you.

Likewise, it's a natural human response for us to react to our kids' emotional outbursts as if they're a threat. That's why it takes a lot for us as parents (and teachers) to keep calm in the face of a dysregulated child - our bodies' automatic reaction is to feel personally attacked and shout in return. But more about that in the next section!

Luckily, shouting isn't the only response we have in our tool-kit. As an adult in this situation, whether an educator or parent, we have three options for how to respond. We can:

1. Swallow their emotions like they're our own, getting equally emotional.
2. Ignore, invalidate or minimize their feelings or sweep them under the rug and pretend they're not there.
3. Perform the two c's: comfort and co-regulate. You help to contain their emotions and provide an anchor for them to weather the storm.

Let's go through each response in turn.

Responding to Emotion With Emotion

It's easy to respond to a child's big emotions by getting equally emotional. After all, intense feelings are uncomfortable to sit with. Some people's automatic response will be to fight fire with fire; to become just as emotional, either by getting upset or angry at the child or the thing that has caused the child's intense emotion.

This is particularly common in adults who find emotional regulation hard, which is often the case for people who have experienced trauma, are very stressed, or are neurodivergent.

It's also a natural human response. If we consider there to be a "threat" (and we register children's emotional outbursts as "threats"), then our stress response is activated, and we begin approaching the situation as a danger to our safety. When your body fills with epinephrine (the stress hormone released during a stress response), your automatic reaction may be to shout or feel personally attacked.

Unfortunately, trying to put out a fire with more fire doesn't work. So, what about sweeping it under the rug?

Ignore, Invalidate, or Minimize

This response is another way of coping with emotions that we find uncomfortable. A child's emotional outburst may be overwhelming because these feelings are unfamiliar to us (if we don't recognize them in ourselves) or if we aren't sure how we can help.

In this instance, we may minimize, invalidate or ignore their feelings to make them "go away." Minimizing involves making something seem less important than it is - this could be "it's not that bad." When someone invalidates another's feelings, they dismiss them, making them seem unimportant or just plain wrong. A common invalidation phrase is, "it could be worse" or "at least it's not XYZ."

Then, there's ignoring the feelings altogether - this could be compared to sweeping dirt under the rug and forgetting about it. This may involve ignoring a child while they're upset, then responding to them when they "cheer up."

Any of these three reactions to a child's intense emotions will result in them continuing the trend. Here's how it works:

1. Child expresses intense emotion.
2. Parent ignores, invalidates, or minimizes.
3. Child assumes their problem isn't bad and it's normal to feel this way. They also learned that they aren't acceptable unless they are regulated.
4. Over time, they no longer respond to the same situation with intense emotion.
5. As an adult, they may ignore, invalidate or minimize their big emotions because we taught them that they were wrong or didn't matter.

So, if the first and second responses aren't effective, what about the two c's - comfort and coregulation?

Comfort and Coregulation

As adults, whether in an educational or parenting capacity, we must contain the young person's big emotions and not bury our heads in the sand or withdraw. When we respond negatively to children's emotional outbursts, we teach them that these emotions aren't acceptable. So, instead of this, we need to teach them that their feelings are valid and how to regulate themselves.

One way to regulate ourselves in these scenarios is to take a moment. Now, it's essential to distinguish between taking a moment and withdrawing. Withdrawing involves removing yourself from the situation because you can't deal with it and leaving the big emotion unresolved. Taking a moment means deciding to leave the situation so that you can regulate yourself before returning to offer comfort and help the child regulate.

Taking a moment for yourself is a valuable tool to have in your inventory. As we said earlier, it's natural to respond to emotion with emotion, so we won't always be in a calm state when a child has an outburst - more than likely, we'll experience dysregulation too. So, how can we take a moment without causing more distress? You can do so by saying something like:

"I know you're really upset/angry/frustrated right now. I'm feeling a little upset/angry/frustrated myself. If we try and have this conversation now, we may both end up feeling worse, so I'm going to take a moment to calm down, and we can work through this together when we're both feeling a little calmer."

By saying something similar to this, you're doing three things:

1. Recognizing their emotion and being open and honest about our emotional state.
2. Reassuring the young person that you're taking a moment for yourself because of the situation, not because of something they have done.

3. Showing care and empathy by telling them that you want to solve the problem and that they're not alone in this.

Only when we are calm can we co-regulate. We have to be in a relaxed headspace to be capable of validating another person's big emotions. Co-regulating with a child helps to show them that they are acceptable whatever their emotion and that they are worthy of another person's love and support.

When a child has had an adult co-regulating with them, they begin to learn how to regulate themselves. We do this through modelling and by showing them that they are worthy. More often than not, when a child sees an adult who is calm and attentive, even in the presence of their big emotions, those feelings begin to lose their intensity.

This proactive and positive approach is particularly useful for neurodiverse children, especially those with ADHD. Teaching these children about gratitude, pride, and compassion - three prosocial emotions - can help them even more when it comes to self-regulation.

You can cultivate gratitude by:

- Sending thank you cards on special occasions
- Taking 5 minutes before bedtime to talk about what you're grateful for that day

- Creating a gratitude jar where the child adds notes into the jar when they're thankful for something
- Complimenting people, including your child, in front of them and encouraging them to compliment people too.
- Noticing when a child shows an act of kindness or goodness and writing it down on an "I noticed" note.

You can build pride by:

- Treat your child as an expert in one of their interests. It doesn't matter what the subject is; allow them space to share their skill and knowledge with you. This could be encouraging them to play their instrument for you or let them teach you about Minecraft.
- Trust your child with an important job. This could be as simple as taking out the trash or picking up the mail. This small act of giving your child responsibility helps them to feel valuable and proud of themself.

And finally, you can demonstrate compassion by:

- Doing a mindfulness meditation together. Meditation is an excellent way for all of us to develop gratitude and compassion, so it's a double whammy.

- Give them lessons on their brain. Children are curious - they love to know how things work. Taking the time to teach them about their developing brain can help them to be compassionate towards themselves when they find something challenging. It may help them to reassure themself that they are still growing and developing.
- Encouraging your child to practice self-compassion. This is an invaluable lesson for children with ADHD because the feedback they tend to get from others is usually negative or that they're doing something wrong. Rather than being hard on themself and berating themself for making a mistake, a child who is self-compassionate can accept that everyone makes mistakes and reassure themself that if they continue to try hard, the desired outcome is likely to come at some point.

Comfort, coregulation, gratitude, pride, and compassion are the building blocks of self-regulation. However, they're not the foundation. The most crucial duty of educators (and parents, for that matter!) is to build a strong relationship with the child.

THE FIRST DUTY OF EDUCATORS LIKE US

I give similar guidance to educators as I do to parents. The first step to take when helping students develop EF skills is to build a solid relationship. A positive teacher-student relationship is the scaffolding each child needs to learn effectively. The relationship has a far bigger impact on student learning than giving them step-by-step instructions or teaching them the curriculum.

From this relationship, your students can develop their social-emotional skills, typically resulting in better learning and higher grades and test scores. It also promotes students' sense of safety - if a child doesn't feel safe, they will not be able to learn.

This boost isn't limited by age, either. Scientific research shows that students from preschool right through to high school significantly improve in educational attainment when they have positive relationships with their teachers (Waterford.org, 2021).

Of course, we all have our triggers, likes, and dislikes. So, naturally, you'll find it easier to form strong bonds with some students than others. This tends to be children who have grown up in stable environments with secure parental relationships. Those who haven't formed strong early attachments to their caregivers may be less responsive to your attempts at a relationship, more hostile, and even rejecting. None of us want to feel rejected, so forming relationships with these kids isn't always easy for us.

It's down to all of us as educators to recognize the need for positive relationships in each and every child and persevere with this through our behavior choices. By doing this, we can form new relationship templates for vulnerable and traumatized children who are perhaps untrusting and suspicious of close relationships. By showing them that we will continue to try to develop a relationship, we show them that they are worthy and deserving of care. This, in itself, is a transformational lesson for any student to learn.

So, how can you build these positive relationships? Here's a simple how-to:

1. Respond to your students with sensitivity and warmth. Take time to respond to each student often and be conscious of how long it's taking you to get to them.
2. If you have a better understanding of the child and how children's brains develop, you'll be able to form a deeper connection with each student. So, do some learning of your own!
3. Show that you have high expectations for each of your students. Your expectations of them will inform their beliefs of their capabilities; this can significantly benefit their confidence and sense of self.
4. Prepare for class. This may seem simple, but your preparation is a surefire sign to your students that you care about their success.
5. Encourage independence by allowing your students to choose wherever possible. Children don't want

you to tell them what to do in every aspect of their learning, all day, every day. If you can give them the flexibility to choose, try to do so.

6. Steer clear of noncoercive interactions. Coercion may be taking away enjoyable activities as a punishment (also called 'punishment by removal'). This doesn't demonstrate that you care; it gives students the exact opposite message, showing a power imbalance and making you the enemy. It also teaches them to be indifferent, so they end up not caring. This isn't a place you want to be!

7. Rather than praising good grades, praise effort. It's not always possible for students to get good grades, but they can try hard. Praising kind behavior is another excellent way to show your students that you think they are "good enough."

The key to these steps is emphasizing the positives, not the negatives. Taking time to value and respect your students will go a long way to building solid relationships and reaching educational outcomes.

In the next chapter, we'll explore how executive dysfunction can disadvantage young people and what assessments are in place to help you pinpoint which children are struggling.

But before assessment comes communication - if you can't communicate with your students, they're unlikely to engage in whatever tasks you give them! One way to help build communication bridges with your students is to teach them about emotions and how to understand their own.

On the next page, you'll find an interactive exercise. You can use this simple tool in the classroom - it'll help your students gauge their emotions and communicate this with you.

Interactive Exercise: Feelings Thermometer

Feelings thermometers are scales that young people can use to identify how they're feeling in the present or how they felt in the past. They can help to build self-awareness, encourage self-management techniques, connect our thoughts with our feelings and actions, and give us a new perspective on a situation.

Anyone using the feelings thermometer will need a basic understanding of feelings like happiness, sadness, anger, and fear. This is the place to start if your students aren't quite there yet. Then, introduce the idea that you can experience feelings in different sizes and intensities.

For example, a student may feel angry when their sibling takes one of their things but only a little annoyed if a friend doesn't choose to play with them at lunchtime. They may feel super duper sad if a relative passes away, but they may only be slightly down if it's raining.

If one thing's true, it's that children will all be on different levels in terms of how comfortable they feel talking about their feelings and how much they understand them. To stick with feelings but make it a little bit less close to home, you can talk about different feelings like a weather forecast. Take a look at the example below for inspiration!

You can create a "feelings thermometer" in many ways - you could use the weather, an inflating and deflating balloon, a tidal wave, and so on. "Zones of Regulation" is also an excellent social-emotional regulation program where you talk about what zone you are in. It is color-coded by emotion. Older students can learn to identify more complicated emotions, as they also experience a rollercoaster of emotions at that age, anyway. The example below is a simple feelings thermometer, but you can search the wide web for what suits your needs best!

3

EXECUTIVE DYSFUNCTION AND ASSESSMENTS

So far, we've talked about "executive function problems" and "executive function difficulties." But there's a specific term - executive dysfunction. In this chapter, we'll learn about the impacts of executive dysfunction on young people and the assessments you can do in class to help you understand their struggles better.

But before all of that, we're going to take a closer look at the three brain areas that are most important when it comes to executive function: working memory, flexible thinking, and inhibitory control.

A CLOSER LOOK AT THE 3 MAIN AREAS OF EF

We know there are three main brain areas associated with EF. But we haven't yet talked much about them. Now, we'll think about precisely what each brain area does and tie this in with the difficulties that come from executive dysfunction. First, up is working memory.

Working Memory

The best way I can describe working memory is like your brain's temporary sticky note. The brain takes in new information, and working memory stores this information in place while the brain is working with it, so you don't forget it. If you keep forgetting the information, you'll likely forget what you're trying to accomplish!

Think about it in terms of a kid answering a question in class. They have to be able to remember the question, even if it's just in the short term, to think about their answer. Without working memory, they wouldn't be able to connect these two things.

That's not the only use working memory has. Just like working memory acts as a temporary sticky note, it also acts as a post office. It helps your brain to sort all of this new information, deciding what's the best way to keep it in your brain for future use. This makes it super easy to retrieve when you next need the information. Once the information is stored long-term, it's like screwing that sticky note up and chucking it in the trash - we no longer need it in our working memory.

Let's now imagine what it's like if this brain area doesn't work correctly. When working memory is dysfunctional, information gets stored in an unorganized, cluttered way, or sometimes not at all! Imagine what it's like when you go to retrieve that information in the future. It'd be like a postal sorting office sending you your mail from yesterday before sending your mail from a month ago! There may even be mail you don't get!

Children struggling with working memory dysfunction may find following a set of instructions hard, or they may get muddled when trying to remember information because it doesn't make sense in their heads. Working memory difficulties are particularly common in people with ADHD.

What about the second brain area, flexible thinking?

Flexible Thinking

Cognitive flexibility is the part of the brain that adapts to new information and situations when things change. It's how your brain can switch between two tasks, also known as task switching.

Let's think of an example. You set group work, and one of your students, let's call him Jack, really wants to work with a particular peer; let's call her Chloe. Unfortunately, Chloe has another idea - she wants to work with Emily. When Chloe pairs up with Emily, Jack has to use his flexible thinking skills to adapt, changing his original idea. In the end, he finds another student who doesn't have a partner and pairs with him.

This is what the situation would look like if Jack had strong, flexible thinking skills. Now, let's consider a Jack with rigid thinking. When Chloe pairs up with Emily, Jack may argue with them because, in his mind, he should pair up with Chloe. If this doesn't end in him working with Chloe, he may refuse to do the task altogether because he finds it hard to see another option. It may take some time and careful explanation on your part for Jack to make an alternative choice.

You see, we use flexible thinking all the time. We use it when multitasking, interacting with others, problem-solving, and concentrating on a task. If you struggle with cognitive flexibility, this will hit you hard in many aspects of life - you may find it challenging to stop doing one task and start another, like continuing with something else after someone you were speaking to leaves abruptly. With flexible thinking skills, you could think about why this person had to go and rationalize their exit. But if you're cognitively inflexible, you may find it really difficult to understand their motivation for leaving.

You'd also likely struggle to solve a problem creatively, especially if you come across some curveballs on the way. It may not just feel like an obstacle to overcome to someone with rigid thinking, but something that makes it impossible to continue.

Now, let's get to the last brain area, inhibitory control. What's this, and what does dysfunction in this area look like?

Inhibitory Control

Inhibitory control sounds pretty complicated, but all it means is self-control. We've all heard of this term, so let's use it here; it's way easier! If we think back to when we were kids or teens, I'm sure we can all agree that our self-control skills weren't the best.

Recently, many parents have been testing their kids' self-control on social media. Have you seen the candy test? Parents leave a piece of candy in front of their kids and tell them that they'll be right back. They say, "if the candy is still there when I get back, I'll give you another piece of candy." This is all about self-control.

The thing is, self-control develops over time, so we're bound to be better at it as adults (even if our self-control is questionable at times - yes, the bag of chips that I wolfed down this week, I'm talking to you!).

What's more, self-control isn't just one skill; it's lots of skills combined. This set of skills helps kids manage their thoughts, feelings, and actions so that they can complete tasks. Here are some everyday examples of scenarios where self-control is essential:

- Waiting in a line
- Sitting still & listening
- Waiting for your turn
- Sharing an item

It's true that kids start building these skills from a young age - parents aren't always able to respond to them instantly, so they have to learn to wait. And if they have siblings, they may have to learn to share from early in life. But as these skills develop, three main areas of self-control evolve:

1. **Movement Control:** This skill stops kids from being hyperactive all the time. It involves being in control of your movements so you're not behaving inappropriately.
2. **Impulse Control:** This skill includes not always giving in to urges and impulses - taking a second to pause and think, "will this benefit me long-term?"
3. **Emotional Control:** This skill enables kids to carry on and persevere even when something unexpected or even upsetting happens.

Self-control is another common difficulty in children with ADHD. These kids often have a harder time than their class-mates managing certain behaviors. You may have seen some of these behaviors in your classroom - they may have even driven you slightly crazy in the past! Here are some common ones:

- **Blurting**
- Spontaneously breaking into song while you're trying to teach.

- Dancing during a lesson, distracting everyone around them.
- Falling off their chair in silent reading, which sends the class into a fit of giggles that requires all your patience to settle!
- **Blurting**
- Snatching things off other students' desks and running away.
- Waving their hand high up in the air, then **blurting** the answer regardless of whether you pick them or someone else.
- Continually clicking their pen lid, playing with rulers, or building towers out of the things on their desks while you're trying to teach the class.
- Did I mention **blurting**?

It may still seem like there's nothing you can do to help these executive function difficulties. After all, they're problems deep down in the brain, right? Wrong! We can do loads of things- and it's not as complicated as you think, I promise! Plus, I'm confident you're already doing many of these strategies without realizing it. But becoming aware of and understanding why we do them will bring more meaning and better results!

EXECUTIVE DYSFUNCTION UNDER THE MICROSCOPE

As we're now aware, executive dysfunction is the name we give when someone struggles with specific skills, including self-control, flexible thinking, and working memory. It's also considered a symptom of conditions that disrupt the brain's ability to regulate our thoughts, feelings, and actions.

I mentioned ADHD earlier - this is one of the most common conditions where you see executive dysfunction. However, other brain-influencing conditions that link to executive dysfunction are:

- Obsessive-Compulsive Disorder (OCD)
- Depression
- Autism Spectrum Disorder
- Addictions (alcohol and drug use)
- Schizophrenia

Executive dysfunction may also occur as a result of brain damage or deterioration. Some of the most common examples of this are stroke, multiple sclerosis, dementia, Alzheimer's disease, brain tumors, and traumatic brain injuries.

And more recent research suggests that COVID may play a role in executive dysfunction. A study found that adults with Severe Acute Respiratory Syndrome Coronavirus 2 (SARS-

CoV-2) reported more executive dysfunction than those who had never had the infection. And the impact on EF increased as symptom severity worsened - people showing worse COVID-19 symptoms displayed more executive dysfunction than mild cases (Hall et al., 2022). Of course, it's early days for this kind of research, so only time will tell the true impact of COVID on executive function.

That's the technical bit over with - phew! Now, let's explore some signs and symptoms of executive dysfunction in general before moving on to classroom-specific signs to look for.

Executive Function Type	Dysfunction Example #1	Dysfunction Example #2
Working Memory	Quickly forgetting directions someone has just given you.	Having to keep looking back at a recipe because you've forgotten the steps.
Flexible Thinking	Repeating a behavior even though you know it is unhelpful and won't get the desired outcome.	Becoming angry, sad, or disappointed when someone doesn't meet an expectation you hold of them.
Task Initiation	Telling yourself, you'll do the dishes *after* this, that, and the other.	Daydreaming when you should be getting started on a task.
Planning, Organizing, Time Management	You do less important tasks first, meaning you don't have enough energy for the most important ones.	You set yourself deadlines that you're unable to meet.
Attention/Focus	Getting distracted while you're midway through one chore - you end up with lots of half-completed tasks.	Focusing so much on something you're reading, you don't hear the doorbell ringing.
Perseverance	Giving up on making a recipe because you don't have one ingredient.	Not continuing to work towards your goals if someone tells you that it's going to be hard.
Self-Reflection	Making excuses when given constructive feedback rather than learning from it.	You find it uncomfortable to say, "I don't know," or "I need help."

So, there are some general signs that you might see in your own life. But what about things to look out for to help identify executive dysfunction in your students? Here's a list to help you out!

Executive Function Type	Dysfunction Example #1	Dysfunction Example #2
Working Memory	Forgetting homework tasks.	Losing their place on a page or during a multi-step task.
Flexible Thinking	Difficulty transitioning from one task to the next.	Changing their workings out in math when they find an answer is wrong.
Task Initiation	Unable to start a task until you speak to them 1-1.	Sharpening their pencil and doodling instead of independently beginning their work.
Planning, Organizing, Time Management	Their desk and backpack are messy and unorganized.	Difficulty estimating the time needed for a task.
Attention/Focus	They always lose their belongings.	They get distracted by something going on out of the window and don't finish their work.
Perseverance	Anxious and overwhelmed when a task is long-winded.	Giving up when they get it wrong.
Self-Reflection	Becoming defensive or combative when you give them a bad grade or constructive criticism.	Repeatedly upsetting their peers because they say hurtful things without considering their friends' feelings.

Have you seen any of these before? As a teacher myself, I can say I've seen my fair share of these examples. When you're not aware of executive function skills, you can quickly become frustrated with children, sometimes believing they're being difficult on purpose! This is rarely the case, and since knowing about executive function, I have been much more empathic and supportive towards the young people in my class.

After all, the behavior is a symptom of something deeper going on. So now, rather than seeing it as a challenge I have to face, I view it as an opportunity to help one of my vulnerable students.

Noticing executive dysfunction in every student is not always easy when you're teaching a class of 20 - 30. But don't worry; that's what EF assessments are for.

FORMAL AND INFORMAL EF ASSESSMENTS

As I'm sure you're well aware, assessments are commonplace in education. However, they can sometimes seem a bit clinical and unforgiving. For executive function, though, they play an essential role in helping us understand a student's strengths and areas that they find challenging.

Once we have this information, we can use it to inform our support strategies. In this way, it's not the assessment that matters but what we do with the result. With focused support strategies, we can help improve our students' confidence in their capabilities, increase their progress, and reduce their anxiety about school and performance.

There are two main types of assessments, each conducted in different ways: formal and informal. Formal assessments follow a grading system - this is usually in the form of a questionnaire. These tend to be performed by healthcare professionals to assess for a clinical diagnosis. Let's look at

10 formal assessments for executive function; then, we'll move on to the informal EF assessment.

Formal EF Assessments

#1 Test of Variables of Attention (TOVA)

As you may have already guessed, this formal assessment measures a child's attention. This is one of the screening assessments used by psychologists and other healthcare professionals to assess for ADHD.

The TOVA is a computer test that is generally just over 10 minutes long for 4 - 5-year-olds and around 22 minutes for anyone older.

The assessment can identify how well a student can stay focused during a tedious task. It also examines their ability to control impulses during a more exciting task. It can distinguish between students who are hyperactive, inattentive, or both.

This test is available either in visual or auditory form. The visual version shows two simple geometric shapes, one being the target shape. The task is to click a switch when the target shape appears and not click when the other shape appears.

The hearing test is the same but with sounds - you click a button when you hear the target sound and don't click when you hear the other sound.

#2 Stroop Color and Word Test

The Stroop test is another assessment of attention, focusing on people's selective attention, processing speed, and overall EF abilities. This test is also carried out by healthcare professionals to help with diagnosis.

The Stroop assessment asks you to name the font color of the word that shows up, not the word itself. The catch is the word will be the name of a color. For example, you may have the word BLUE written in red or BLUE written in blue.

Of course, if the color and the word are the same, these are easier to get right. But when the word and the color don't match, this is where the real test is - can you ignore the written word and concentrate on the font color? Many people find this tricky, but more so if they have executive dysfunction.

Professions can assess both children and adults using the Stroop test. It takes just 5 minutes to complete.

#3 Digit Span and Spatial Span (WISC)

These are digital tests assessing working memory. They're usually conducted by healthcare professionals. Still, you don't need any qualifications to administer them, so they could be a good way of getting an idea of your students' working memory abilities.

The Digit Span test comes in two formats: Forward Digit Span and Reverse Digit Span. For the Forward Digit Span test, you have to try and remember a number sequence that appears, one number appearing after the other, in the order that it occurred. Each time you get it right, the sequence will increase in length by one digit. If you get it wrong, your number sequence will get shorter. Then, if you get it wrong three times in a row, the assessment ends.

Reverse Digit Span is the same concept, but you repeat the sequence backward. So, say the series was 5 7 9 2 6 3. The correct answer would be 3 6 2 9 7 5. This test takes up to 3 minutes to complete.

The Spatial Span test is very similar to the Digit Span test. In this test, squares show on the screen, one after the other, each displaying a color. The child has to remember this sequence of colors until the end. Then, when the series finishes, the child is asked to touch each of the colored boxes in the order that they showed on the screen. The sequence starts with just two boxes, increasing by one every time the child gets it right and decreasing every time the child gets it wrong.

This test takes up to 5 minutes to complete.

#4 Conners 3

This assessment tool is slightly different from the ones we've discussed. How so? Well, it bases the assessment on parents' observations of their children. This test assesses ADHD in children aged 6 to 18 years. Healthcare professionals frequently use this alongside other assessment tools to diagnose ADHD.

It's a questionnaire that measures several aspects of ADHD, including:

- Impulsivity
- Social skills
- Attention problems
- Defiant behavior
- Learning difficulties

When a professional evaluates the completed questionnaire, they'll look out for whether the ratings are within the normal range for the child's age group or whether they fall above or below the expectation.

A teacher version of the Conners 3 assessment is also available. As educators supporting a child, we can fill this out and evaluate the scores. Of course, we can't use this to diagnose anyone with a health condition, but it can help us to identify where someone may need additional support.

It can be completed online or on paper and takes around 20 minutes.

#5 Behavior Rating Inventory of Executive Function (BRIEF)

The BRIEF is another questionnaire that parents or teachers complete. It assesses a child or adolescent's executive function behaviors in school or at home.

This tool is helpful when assessing a child with a learning difficulty, attention disorder, developmental disorder, mood disorder, or other medical condition because it provides multiple perspectives on where the child is struggling.

It measures several executive function skills, including:

- Inhibition
- Attention shifting
- Emotional Control
- Task initiation
- Working memory
- Planning & organizing
- Self-monitoring

The standard version of this test can assess children between 5 and 18 years old. However, there is also a preschool version (BRIEF-P) and a self-report version (BRIEF-SR) for 11 - 18-year-olds working at a fifth-grade reading level or above.

It typically takes between 10 and 15 minutes to complete the BRIEF, BRIEF-P, and BRIEF-SR assessments.

#6 Wechsler Intelligence Scale for Children - 5th Edition (WISC-IV)

The latest edition of the WISC assessment, the WISC-IV, is the gold standard of EF assessments. This testing tool assesses general intellectual performance in 6 - 16-year-old children, including:

- **Verbal comprehension:** how well a child listens to a question, uses learned information, figures out the answer, and expresses this out loud.
- **Perceptual reasoning:** how well a child can look at a problem, analyze it using their visual skills, organize their thoughts, and problem-solving.
- **Working memory:** how well a child holds new information in short-term memory, concentrates, and uses this information to help them through a problem.
- **Processing speed:** how well a child focuses attention, quickly scans information, chooses essential bits of information, and orders visual information. This requires perseverance and planning.

This test measures intellectual performance rather than general intelligence because it doesn't matter how intelligent you are unless you know how to use that to improve and adapt to the environment. In other words, intellectual performance is all about how a child uses their intelligence, whereas general intelligence is about how intelligent they are.

This test is a little longer than most, taking around 45 - 65 minutes to complete. Clinicians often use the WISC-IV to diagnose ADHD and learning difficulties. However, you can also use it in class to create focused learning plans for children requiring a little more support. As I'm sure every teacher knows (because it's drummed into our heads all the time!), we can't use this to diagnose a child with any medical condition.

Informal EF Assessments

Informal assessments don't follow a graded system, making them much more based on self-report and evaluation. You could use observation, a checklist, or even a 1-1 activity as an informal EF assessment. What's great about these assessment tools is that they're suitable for any age - you can adapt them however you want to fit the age group you're working with.

If you're using observation as your informal EF assessment, consider how your students perform when doing the following tasks:

- Beginning an action (task initiation)
- Coming up with ideas to do an action (planning)

- Organizing their belongings, including learning materials (organization)
- Working through a whole step before moving on to another one (attention, impulse control)
- Switching their behaviors and thinking between steps (flexible thinking)
- Coming up with tactics for a game or problem-solving activity (flexible thinking, planning)
- Thinking of different ways to solve a problem (problem-solving, shifting, flexible thinking)
- Holding information in mind as they answer questions or complete a task (working memory)
- Regulating their emotions and behaviors to deal with changes in demand (working memory)

You can also think about a child's distraction levels (attention), whether they lose track of their belongings (working memory), and if they're able to wait for their turn (self-control).

Alternatively, if you'd prefer a checklist to work from, you can use the one provided below! This is an executive function-specific worksheet that focuses on performance and academic challenges that are related to ADHD. This can help you identify a student's difficulties, allowing you to develop a targeted support plan.

Interactive Element: Executive Function Checklist

▷ **Performance Challenges**

Starting a task and persevering until it's complete

- Use visual reminders such as sticky notes or a timer.
- Use auditory reminders such as an adult prompt or an alarm.
- Give a subtle signal to remind them it's time to start the task, e.g., touching your chin.

Following directions

- Give step-by-step instructions on a 1-1 basis.
- Provide written step-by-step instructions for the student on their desk.
- Break steps down into smaller, more manageable chunks.

Being organized

- Model how students can tidy and organize their workspaces by organizing your desk.
- Asking a peer to help a student organize their belongings.
- Staff weekly support to organize workbooks and desk/cubby.

Time-management

- Have a student set themselves a timer that counts down the time they should be working on a task.
- Model time-management skills by talking through how long it will take for you to do certain things.
- Encourage parents to show time-management skills by getting students to school on time.

Remembering to complete homework and hand it in on time

- Students can make a plan on when they are going to do their homework in their planner.
- Students can write down notes in their planners so parents can check if they have any homework to do.
- Students will use sticky notes to write down when homework is due.

Showing appropriate self-control

- Visual timetable of how to put your hand up and respond to questions a teacher asks the class.
- Rewarding appropriate self-control using a bump-it-up wall.
- Verbal reminders for students to put their hands up and wait their turn.

▷ **Academic Challenges**

Remembering important information

- Appoint a note taker to model how to take notes.
- Provide a hand-out with the most important bits of information highlighted in a bright color.
- Write the most important points on sticky notes.

Remembering facts, including multiplication tables, math formulas, and letters

- Using memory tricks like chunking and acronyms.
- Provide hand-outs of multiplication tables and math formulas that students can keep on their desks or in their cubbies.
- Teach using physical objects like counting cubes.

Persevering with long-term projects

- Give students graphic organizers for them to plan the steps they need to take to complete the project.
- Give each student a job card of their responsibilities.
- Break long-term goals into lots of smaller, short-term goals with deadlines for each.

Working through challenging math, like algebra

- Go through the first question together, showing the workings out on the board so students can copy the method.
- Give each student a handout with the first question filled out, showing how you reached the answer.
- Allow students to work in pairs, helping each other to come to the correct answer.

Slow processing speed

- Allow some students more time depending on their processing speed.
- Give students with slow processing speed shortened tasks so they can complete the task in the same amount of time as their peers.
- Skip the part where students write down the question, providing them with hand-outs, so all they need to do is write the answers.

Completing written work/assignments

- Talk through the task as a class, brainstorming ideas before students work on the task independently.
- Provide a scribe for students that struggle with attention difficulties.

- Give students graphic organizers with a walkthrough of the steps needed to complete the task.

HOW WE TEACHERS CAN EXPLORE OUR WEAKNESSES

I know what you're thinking - uh oh! No one really wants to delve deep into their weaknesses and pick themselves apart. While we will be looking at the things we can work on in this section, we won't criticize ourselves silly.

So, what's the purpose of discovering our weaknesses? As teachers, we have a duty to practice as we preach. We shouldn't tell our students to do anything we wouldn't be willing to do ourselves, including building on our self-awareness. By doing this, we become role models for our students, showing them the ideal behavior.

Luckily, as educators, we quite naturally reflect. We see progress in a student and recognize that we have a part to play in this. We can also tell when a lesson plan doesn't go as we wanted it to or when a method for regulating student behaviors had the exact opposite effect.

While this form of reflection is important, it's not the same as purposeful self-reflection and self-evaluation. Self-reflection is a more habitual and systematic process, taking time and energy to see personal growth. But just like assessments help you to identify focused support plans for your students, actively evaluating yourself enables you to identify your EF skills, including areas of weakness.

You may ask, "why do I need to evaluate my EF skills?" It's good to know your executive function strengths and weaknesses because this can help you identify why a lesson went well (or not so swimmingly!).

For example, if a lesson didn't go to plan and you know you struggle with time management, you may ask yourself, "was it because I didn't manage my time effectively?" or "did I give my students enough time to do everything well?"

You can also use your knowledge about your executive function skills, like attention, to your advantage. For instance, put yourself in your student's shoes and ask, "was the content dry and hard to pay attention to? Could I have concentrated through that?"

Finally, consider whether you provided pictures to help your non-verbal learners follow along - was there anything else you could have done to keep them engaged? Working through each one of the EF skills can help massively when trying to identify what went wrong.

And that's not the only benefit. Self-evaluation is also helpful because it:

- Helps you uncover difficulties you previously overlooked
- Is tailored specifically to you and your needs

- Encourages you to be honest about things that work in the classroom and things that don't!
- Demonstrates you're working hard in your educator role
- Can benefit you in all aspects of life, including professionally, in relationships, and self-confidence.

So, how can you reflect on and evaluate yourself? The first and easiest step to take is to start asking yourself curious questions, the two most important being:

1. What's gone well?
2. What's not gone well?

You can also ask yourself teacher-specific questions if these are too broad. Here are some examples:

- What was my major win in this unit?
- When have I loved teaching?
- When haven't I loved teaching?
- What's my work/life balance like?
- What are my strengths in my teaching role?
- What are the main struggles in my teaching role?
- When have I felt proud of myself in this unit?
- What were my favorite times in this unit?
- How did I overcome this goal's challenges?

Once you've done that, it's time to set some goals. You can do this by asking yourself another set of questions:

- Which teachers do I admire most?
- How could I reach out to these to mentor me?
- What are the three main areas where I have room for improvement?
- What skills would I like to work on in the upcoming term?
- What would a "great week" look and feel like?

When answering each question, be as specific as possible because this will help you remain focused throughout the following semester. Honesty is just as, if not more important, as being specific because being honest is a vital part of evaluating yourself. If you're not honest with yourself, how can you grow?

Finally, don't rush your self-reflection. Take time. It may not always feel comfortable, but that's when you know you're hitting on something emotive. Maybe you feel uncomfortable about your weaknesses - you aren't the only one! We would all be perfect if we could. Make sure you're in a space that feels safe, comforting, and free from distractions, as this helps you get in the zone.

You can try this task once a semester or any time you want to. It's great to get in the habit of self-reflecting regularly because then you'll start doing it automatically without the need for paper and pen.

THE RECIPROCAL BOND BETWEEN EF AND LANGUAGE

At first glance, it may not seem like there's much of a bond between executive function and language. But there is, in fact, a deep relationship between the two because language isn't just about speaking to others and hearing their response. It also helps us to form an "internal script" in our minds. You may have noticed this before - perhaps you found yourself questioning your thoughts or actions or criticizing yourself for thinking or doing certain things. The internal dialogue helps us reflect, but it also enables us to plan, monitor, and execute the tasks we complete daily. We call this internal script "metacognition."

While metacognition seems pretty automatic and natural in many of us, it's not that way for those with executive dysfunction because their language skills tend to be underdeveloped.

This isn't very easy to understand without an example, so let's go straight into one. We'll talk about Daniel, a 10-year-old student with executive dysfunction.

- **Reading Comprehension:** Daniel is reading one of the set books for his English class. To read well, he needs to do several things: focus on the book, use his working memory to decode and make sense of new words, and combine his existing knowledge with new information. Daniel is also using flexible thinking and problem-solving to predict what's going to happen next and use the content he has read as context to help him read the words he doesn't know.

- **Auditory Comprehension:** Daniel is in math class. He listens to his teacher when they talk about algebra, continually paying attention so that he'll know what to do when he has to do independent work. He has to ignore distracting noises from his classmates, process the language his teacher is using, and identify the most important information so that he can write it down.

- **Oral Language:** Daniel learns a new song in music class. He has to listen to the song, store this new information in his working memory, and then organize, plan, and sequence it in his mind so he can repeat it when asked. If he's unable to do this, he will likely sing the words in the wrong order or forget the tune. As he sings, he has to be able to identify whether the teacher understands what he's singing. If they don't, he has to adapt, requiring flexible thinking.

- **Written Language:** Daniel has been asked to write about his summer break. He needs to prioritize and sequence the content, so it comes out in an organized, coherent order. He also needs to bring many pieces of information together to form a well-written piece. He needs to be able to switch from writing about one activity to writing about something else, requiring flexibility. He needs to use self-monitoring and problem-solving when checking over his work so that he can edit it.

While it may not seem like it, to begin with, you can't have executive function without language, and vice versa. The bond's reciprocal. Now, you can see the massive detrimental effect executive dysfunction can cause, not just on practical skills like taking turns and planning but also on communication and language.

We've covered so much of executive function in this chapter. We've thought about examples for each EF skill and how you can assess them. Next, we'll look at how you can integrate these essential skills into your classroom, starting with planning, organizing, and time management.

But before we wrap up chapter 3 completely, here are some self-report handouts you can give your students to help you better understand their executive function needs.

Interactive Element: Classroom Assessment Tool for EF Skills

Planning, Organizing, Time Management

Check the boxes that are true for you.

❏ I always under or overestimate how long things will take

❏ Everything comes out in a jumbled order

❏ I struggle to identify the steps I need to take to reach a goal

❏ I often do less important tasks before really important tasks

❏ I find it hard to hand my homework in on time

Working Memory

Check the boxes that are true for you.

❏ I forget a question before I've figured out the answer

❏ I can't remember instructions the teacher has just told me

❏ When I'm reading, I often forget where I am on the page

❏ When I tell stories, the information comes out all jumbled up

❏ I stop completing a task because it's too hard to remember all the information

Flexible Thinking

Check the boxes that are true for you.

❏ I get confused when a situation changes quickly
❏ If something doesn't go the way I expect it to, I don't know what to do
❏ When people don't act like I think they're going to, I get emotional (sad/angry/annoyed)
❏ It's overwhelming when I'm asked to change what I'm doing midway through
❏ I get frustrated when little things go wrong
❏ I get upset when other people don't go by the rules
❏ I don't like new schedules

Task Initiation

Check the boxes that are true for you.

❏ It takes me a long time to get started on a task
❏ I like to find other things to do rather than completing my work
❏ I need 1-1 help from the teacher to start a task
❏ I become easily distracted when it's time to start a task
❏ I get anxious about starting something because I want it to be perfect

4

PLANNING, ORGANIZING, AND TIME MANAGEMENT

I can safely say we've all experienced a day when planning went out the window; this likely ended up with children not getting much done and everything taking longer than it should have. The probable cause was that misunderstanding the students in the class, including their EF needs.

The thing is, you could be the most organized educator in the world, having planned your lessons to within an inch of their lives, but if you don't know your students or your students struggle with executive dysfunction, you end up like a fish swimming against the current. And on the most disastrous days, it may feel like you're a fish plucked straight out of the water!

So, what can you do about it? In this chapter, we'll go through what it's like to be in a classroom where planning, organization, and time management are nowhere to be seen. Then, we'll see the crazy difference of bringing these essential executive function skills into your classroom, including the impact this has on you and your students.

WHEN THE WORST HAPPENS: NO PLANNING IN THE CLASSROOM

Planning is heavily pushed in the teaching profession, and there's a good reason for this. The teacher's planning gives structure and confidence. Without it, students lose focus and their precious learning time (and your all-too-important teaching time!) goes to waste.

I've experienced so many pressures as an educator, so when I talk about planning, I'm not saying it on a pedestal. There have been occasions where I, too, have skipped the planning stage or simply forgotten to do it with everything else going on. All of us have done it, so don't be hard on yourself if there are times when your planning hasn't been up to scratch. We're all human at the end of the day.

The problem with falling behind on planning is that it's much harder to keep track of students' progress, which can leave you, and them unmotivated. You also won't know if your students are hitting their goals, which is a tricky business when you've got your own goals to meet. I honestly believe that planning is the bread and butter of teaching - it helps me be a successful teacher and keeps me sane and enthusiastic.

Here are some of the strategies I take to make sure I'm planning lessons effectively:

- **Check your teaching content to the curriculum:** Experts have already spent time and energy on making goals and lesson ideas, plus it's mandatory! We all have used random worksheets that fill in time but is it useful time and what are you and the students getting out of it? Curriculum's are based on scaffolding from year to year. That's why I always, always check my teaching content - it's virtually impossible to go wrong this way!
- **Keep track of your progress:** Use tools like lesson plans to keep yourself on track during lessons - we all find ourselves going off on a tangent sometimes! If you find yourself off-topic, you can check back on your lesson plan and carry on as planned. You can also share these with your colleagues. Be proud of the units you did awesome in and evaluate other units that require more attention to detail next time.
- **Create student-oriented planning:** There's no point in planning a lesson that won't work with the kids in your class. If you have a class of hyperactive kids, give them a hands-on task to prevent fidgeting and keep them engaged. Put yourself in your students'

shoes - if you aren't having fun, they most certainly won't!

- **Use your flexible thinking:** There's no guarantee that a lesson plan will work out, no matter how badly we want it to. Be prepared to abandon an exercise if it really isn't turning out well, and think on your feet. In these moments, remember the priorities (learning objectives and skills) and ensure your students grasp these at the very least.
- **Stick to the same structure:** We humans all like a certain element of predictability, school-age children included. Of course, the material will change for each lesson, but that doesn't mean the structure has to be massively different each time. Providing consistency for your students will allow them to get themselves in the mindset to learn. Not to mention it'll save you time coming up with different lesson structures!

With this last point in mind, in particular, that's not to say that lessons should be the same. I'm a big advocate of trying something new rather than always sticking with the tried and tested methods. That's another massive gem that planning unlocks. When you plan your lessons, you can be creative and innovative. You can throw in new ideas and see what sinks and what swims.

And if you still need an extra nudge towards planning, think of it as an opportunity to practice self-monitoring and self-reflection! Planning will help you to become a better teacher and learn more about yourself!

But that's just one side of planning. The second is physical planning - planning your classroom layout and how you will set up your space to get maximum results. Now, this won't apply to everyone because some teachers move from class to class, particularly those who work in specialist provisions. But for those of us who have our classroom, we need to think about our classroom SPACE.

Here are some tips to change up your space and make way for more learning:

- **Move your desk so it's not a focal point:** This may seem like a strange tip, but hear me out. Make the space student-focused. Moving your desk to the back can create more space for learning while keeping all of your students in sight.
- **Don't keep changing the space:** Familiarity feels safe for children and young people, just like it does for us adults! Keeping the classroom layout consistent helps your students develop ownership of their workstations.
- **Switch things around to suit a lesson's needs:** You don't have to keep a consistent layout for every lesson. If a foreign language lesson would benefit from students sitting in a circle, give that a go! Or if a

lesson requires group work, have your students move their tables together to form small groups!

- **Separate active and quiet zones:** Some classrooms call for quiet areas as well as those active and alive with learning. Ensure you separate the two by creating different zones. You can use furniture, signs, and displays to make the distinction.

What other ways can you bring planning into your classroom? Let's take a look in the next section!

HOW TO SPRINKLE PLANNING INTO YOUR CLASSROOM

In this section, we whizz through lots of handy tools you can use to bring planning into your classroom. I love these techniques because they're quick to prepare and easy to implement. Let's go!

Checklists

Checklists allow children to take responsibility and feel more in control of their learning. It can also help students understand processes more - they can use these organization tools to break down the steps needed to complete a task, like a written assignment.

It's also super easy to see your progress if you use checklists, which can be a natural motivator for children struggling to stay on task.

You can encourage your students to use checklists by bringing them into your lessons, demonstrating how they work by completing a list together, and then giving them the time and freedom to create their own. For those who will find this tough, have samples ready to use.

Concept Mapping

Concept maps are visual organizers that bring multiple elements of a concept together to help students understand how they relate to each other. Concept maps are very common in Science, particularly for topics like life cycles, but they are so flexible they can be used in absolutely any area!

Allowing your students to create their concept maps can help them to organize their thoughts and ideas about a topic. For example, you could get them to write down all of the resources they need to be a successful learner in a concept map. You can then help them cluster ideas, focusing on what resources they need for which lessons, what items are essential all the time, and which you only need every now and then.

But if you're going to use concept maps as a learning aid, always, always remember to introduce what they are and model how to create one. While this will be old news for some kids and they'll likely roll their eyes when you begin your explanation, others won't have a clue of what a concept map is. To give all of your students an equal chance of building these skills, show them how to use these helpful tools!

Get your students to do concept maps before a writing task, before organizing their desks, cubby, or locker, or to identify what skills they need to be effective learners.

Concept mapping is particularly beneficial for children who struggle with working memory, as it's a visual tool to help them organize new information.

Keeping the Correct Supplies

We all know one student who always asks for a pen or a ruler. Of course, you could just give them the pen, as we often do, and be done with it. But this doesn't solve the problem - you'll just need to keep a pen handy!

Having the right equipment can make the difference between starting a lesson on time and being five minutes behind everyone else. For children with executive dysfunction, this may mean they miss the all-important starter exercise and are constantly playing catch up.

So, if we can prevent this, we should. It's good practice for educators to teach their students what resources they need rather than assuming that they already know. While we'll often provide the supplies, students must understand what they'll need to be ready to learn each lesson. If they know what they need, they'll think, "it's math; let me get out my pencil, ruler, and eraser," or "it's time for English; I'm going to need a black pen."

The key is to check that they've got the right equipment throughout the year because children lose and forget things more and more as the year progresses, so it's likely that they will be missing important bits of equipment unless you pull them up on it. Often, when we're clearing up for the day, we find these odds and sods lying around, not packed away. Keep a lost and found box in the classroom with all the supplies left around.

Using a Calendar or Agenda

Calendars and agendas are an essential way to encourage students to build their organizational and time-management skills. With their calendar or schedule on their desk, they can check back on any reminders they've made for homework and keep track of their progress toward goals. Make sure you have a class one to model for and with them! Using a monthly calendar in tandem with a weekly calendar promotes planning ahead and how to juggle soccer practice with reading calendar and a math test etc.

Students can use planners to write down checklists, including to-do lists, to help them keep focused. Like check-lists, this little tool breeds independence, allowing them to take more responsibility for their learning.

Graphic Organizers

Graphic organizers are a vital scaffold that all teachers can use to support their students' learning, regardless of age. Just like concept maps, graphic organizers help students to organize all kinds of information and identify relationships between different elements.

They're an awesome way to simplify complex information and provide a visual aid when verbal explanations seem confusing. Moreover, this tool helps to move new information from short-term to long-term memory, making abstract concepts much more concrete in their minds.

You can also provide your students with empty graphic organizers. This will help them identify the most important bits of information, which can guide their note-taking process. It can also help keep them engaged, rather than giving them a handout already filled out.

Provide Rubrics

Rubrics are a tool that allows you to assess your students' work. They're a scoring guide that outlines what you're looking for students to do to achieve the best possible scores.

This is an essential step if you want to increase your students' self-monitoring skills, as rubrics allow you to structure your observations of a student's work in a way that makes it easy for them to see the strengths and weaknesses in their work. This helps them to identify what areas they need to work on, giving them a clear goal to aim for in future assessments.

To get your students involved with rubrics, allow them to mark each other's work using a rubric you provide. This can really help them to get to grips with marking criteria, allowing them to see first-hand what they need to do to get better scores.

WHY CREATING AN ORGANIZED SPACE IS SUPER IMPORTANT

We've talked about planning. Next on the list is organization. Organization is all about how we bring things together in our environment to finish tasks quickly and efficiently.

When we organize ourselves, we bring order and structure to our immediate environment, including our belongings and activities. As I'm sure you can guess, organization shares a close bond with planning.

Without any organization, our world would quickly turn chaotic. This is the same for our students. When the learning space is unorganized, more distractions are present to steer students away from learning. This brings more stress and ultimately leads to challenges academically, including lower grades and bad teacher-student relationships. And we know the importance of this relationship because we talked about it previously!

What's more, problem behaviors are more likely to occur in children with executive dysfunction and other health conditions if exposed to an unorganized learning space. When everything's organized, it feels like we're in control. But when there's no organization, things can quickly get away from us, which is when problem behaviors may arise.

Luckily, there are signs you can look out for that indicate a student is struggling with poor organizational skills. Here are some of the main ones:

- They forget the essential equipment like a pen, pencil, or ruler.
- They lose or forget their homework or don't hand it in on time.
- Their desk, cubby, or locker is a real mess.
- They become hyperactive, fidgety, or agitated when one class ends and another begins.

As educators, we can model organization. We can also directly teach our students techniques to organize themselves, so they can build these skills and step away from the chaos. We go over ways to do this next.

HOW YOU CAN BECOME AN ORGANIZATIONAL ROLE MODEL

You can become an organizational role model by checking you have the suitable systems in place - plain and simple. So, what are the most important systems to keep in check? Let's take a look.

Student Supplies

The system for organizing student supplies is the most important one for me because it saves me from an endless onslaught of questions - "Where do I hand this in?" "I don't have a pencil!" But more to the point, it gives your students more independence and control over their learning, which is invaluable.

There are some bits of equipment that every student needs, either daily or at one point or another. You can demonstrate how neatly these things fit into a pencil case to show how they can keep all their supplies together - this will reduce the risk of losing something important.

Then, help your students to organize their books and bits of loose paper in color-coded folders. Binders, by the way, are shown to not be successful for those with ADHD but color coded folders seem to have more success. Give students a book bin or a cubby of sorts, and make sure their books go back in once they've finished a class.

As much as we'd absolutely love to be so organized that students never have to ask for a pencil, calculator, or tissue again, that's unrealistic. Have those lost & found bins clearly marked so students can independently get one if they need it. But if you encourage your students to stay organized, it'll definitely bring the instances of this right down. Give time for them to organize their spots. You'll have happier, more independent students, and you'll have more time on your hands!

Desk Organization

Then, there's desk organization! Organization is the key that unlocks productivity. Students with tidy desks are less likely to get distracted by junk. The likelihood of losing their all-important equipment is also far smaller when they can see everything on their desk. This leaves more time for learning and effective learning at that!

And the benefits go deeper than that - evidence shows that students show better posture when they sit at an organized desk. When there's clutter, students tend to slump.

So, how can your students organize their desks? The first step is to get all items that aren't essential for learning away from their workstation area.

Then comes the actual desk. You can ensure that messy desks are no more by following 3 simple steps:

1. Model the desk

The first step is to model a perfect desk, either by using your own or bringing another desk to the front as an example. Ensure all the essentials are stacked neatly or in a pencil case.

Show an example of perfectly color-coded books. Allow them to copy this so that their books are color-coded in the same way. This method is particularly beneficial for kids with ADHD as they don't typically get along with binders. You can also provide different coloured folders to match the books so they know where to keep any additional handouts and homework tasks.

2. Do a morning desk check

There's no point in going through the whole process of modeling the perfect desk if you're not going to follow through with the process. Start the day by checking over their supplies to make sure they have got what they need, then, over time, allow them to do this themselves. Give them a gentle reminder each morning so that it becomes a habit naturally.

3. Partner them up

Get your students to check their neighbor's desk. Tell them to show you a thumbs up if it's neat and tidy or a thumbs down if they're unhappy with how it looks. This can be a short, 30-second activity that you can do at the end of your last lesson each day.

If the desk isn't up to standard, the partners work together to get the desk back in order. Doing this ensures everyone will be ready to learn in the morning.

TICK, TICK, TICK: THE IMPORTANCE OF TIME MANAGEMENT

Time is your only non-renewable resource in the classroom. Once it's gone, there's no way of getting it back. It'll only add stress to your day if you continually try to play catchup.

We've all seen students with poor time-management skills - particularly kids with ADHD. They're cool as a cucumber, to begin with, assuming that they have all of the time in the world to get a task done. They fall into the habit of thinking, "I have lots of time."

But they rarely have as much time as they believe they do. By the time they realize they're running out of time, it's not long until the deadline. That's when the rush of panic comes - they think, "I have to do this right now," and nothing can get in the way. They work on the task like mad, often causing the result to not make much sense because of the stress fueling them to get it done. Work completed under these conditions is very rarely their best.

There's no need for this cycle of procrastination followed by stress. Supporting your students to build on their time-management skills will help them to avoid this unhealthy and anxiety-provoking cycle.

And the benefits don't end there. Once students organize their time effectively, they'll begin to see that they spend less time on their work because they're giving short bursts of undivided attention rather than long periods of distraction. This frees up more time for enjoyable things like seeing their friends and watching their favorite shows.

HOW TO TEACH YOUR STUDENTS TIME MANAGEMENT SKILLS

A Visual Timetable and an Analog Clock

One way to improve your students' time-management skills is to say good bye to the idea of "now" and "not now" in the classroom. You can do this using visual timetables and an analog clock. If you teach your students to understand that at 9 AM on Tuesday, you do math, or at noon you have lunch, all you have to say is, "look what time it is on the clock," and they can figure out what they need to do for themselves.

Personal calendars and agendas are also awesome tools to help your students manage their time more effectively. But remember to constantly teach your students how to use these resources rather than assuming they already know. This will prevent planners, calendars, and agendas from sitting on their desks or in their cubby or locker, unopened, for the inevitable future!

The Pomodoro Technique

The Pomodoro Technique is my go-to tool when I notice a student often gets distracted, struggles to remain focused for a set time, and finds time management challenging. University student Francesco Cirillo developed this technique in the last 1980s to help him focus on completing his work. So, what did he do?

He told himself to focus on his work for just 10 minutes. He picked up a tomato-shaped kitchen timer, set it to 10 minutes, and got to work. This method worked wonders for him, and it's shown to be awesome when you apply it to younger students, too. Here's how it goes:

1. Get your students to write a to-do list for themselves.
2. Set a timer for 25 minutes for children aged 11+ (or a 10-minute time for children younger than this) and encourage them to focus on their to-do list and to-do list alone until they hear the timer ring.
3. When the timed session ends, mark off one complete Pomodoro and jot down what you managed to complete.
4. Give yourself a 5-minute reward break!
5. Repeat the process for four Pomodoros, then take a longer, 15-30 minute break.

If any of your students become distracted, remind them of the task and let them get back on track. If there's a disruption that you couldn't possibly avoid, like a fire alarm, take a break and resume when you can.

Try it out and see the improvement in the attention of your students!

Time-Management Games

There are games for every executive function skill, including time management! For this particular skill, the best of the bunch are:

- **The jigsaw puzzle:** Put your students into groups of 3 - 5. Give each group a puzzle without giving them the big picture of the image showing what it'll look like when the puzzle is finished. After 3 minutes, pause your students and ask them, "what's missing?" When they inevitably say that they can't see the big picture, hand them the picture and allow them to complete their puzzles. Have a discussion after about how difficult it is to work quickly and efficiently when you don't know what the end goal is.
- **How long is a minute?** Ask your students to stand up and close their eyes. Tell them that you're going to set a timer of one minute, and when they think the minute is over, they should sit down. Tell them to do this quietly, so their classmates don't hear them. When everyone has sat down, you can use this to start a chat about why people sit down at different times.
- **The mayo jar:** Bring a big mayo jar into the classroom, along with a load of large rocks, small rocks, and other

smaller items like gravel and sand. Also, prepare a jug of water. The task you set your students is to get all the items into the jar. The only way you can do this is to start with the biggest items and progressively get smaller and smaller. Once your students have cracked it, talk to them about the importance of prioritizing.

Now you know how to teach your students planning, organization, and time management, the last piece of the puzzle is supporting them to stop procrastinating.

ENOUGH IS ENOUGH: PUTTING A STOP TO PROCRASTINATION

Planning, organization, and time management are all linked to procrastination. We procrastinate to avoid a task that we have negative feelings towards. Perhaps it brings on feelings of boredom, inadequacy, anxiety, frustration, and so on. This is what we call "task aversion" - when we see a task as unpleasant because we view it in a negative light and anticipate it bringing negative feelings.

The problem with procrastination is that it only increases our stress levels. There's evidence to prove it! A 2019 study by Sara Laybourn and colleagues found that, out of 27 German teachers, 16 often procrastinated (Laybourn et al., 2019). In those 16, this led to negative emotions and higher stress levels.

So, how many of our students procrastinate? All it takes is a little teaching experience to realize that procrastination is something that most students do regularly. In fact, evidence shows that anywhere between 80 and 95% of college students procrastinate.

What can we, as educators, do about it? We can help our students to overcome procrastination in 5 simple steps.

1. Encourage students to get in the know about their procrastination

Help your students to think about why they procrastinate. You can use concept maps to get them to brainstorm ideas. Ask them why they try to avoid a particular task - do they think it will be boring? Hard? Cause anxiety?

Then ask them what they do when they procrastinate. Do they look out the classroom window? Do they start chatting away with their neighbor? Perhaps they lob things across the classroom, distracting everyone around them. When it comes to older children and homework, do they go on social media? Watch Netflix shows? Eat?

Be sure to support students to help them identify their procrastination activities if they need it because some may not have even noticed their procrastination patterns!

Whatever their preferred form of procrastination, getting in the know about what they do and how they become distracted can help them to avoid this in the future.

2. Tell students that is the new perfect

Remind your students that perfect isn't achievable. Searching for perfection just adds way too much weight to their shoulders, making them more likely to procrastinate.

You can help stop your students from feeling overwhelmed, stressed, and anxious by continually:

- Reminding your students to ask themselves, "is this the best I can do?"
- Getting them to self-evaluate their work with a rubric.
- Bringing their attention to the bump-it-up wall.

As a result, they'll complete the task.

3. Help students to get smart with "SMART" goals

While normal, long-term goals can be overwhelming and anxiety-provoking for young people, SMART goals seem to have the opposite effect. They break down the goal-reaching process, allowing students to see little wins as they get closer and closer to their long-term aim.

SMART stands for:

- **Specific:** Get your students to be clear about what they want to achieve - no wishy-washy language that makes it to get out of achieving their goal.
- **Measurable:** You need to be able to measure a goal for it to be effective, so ask your students to set themselves a time limit. For example, a measurable goal could be "write 300 words in 1 hour."
- **Achievable:** Check that your students have control over meeting their goal - if they're relying on someone else to achieve their goal, they can't be sure they'll complete it within their deadline.
- **Realistic:** Encourage your students to set goals for themselves that they can actually achieve in the time frame. Otherwise, they'll end up losing confidence and feeling defeated.
- **Time-oriented:** Make sure they set themselves a deadline because this will help them to focus and avoid procrastination.

SMART goals will give your students a clear line of focus and set them on the path to success.

4. Remind students to be kind to themselves

Sometimes, unavoidable things get in the way of achieving our goals. And at other times, we just don't manage to achieve them, despite everything going out way.

It's common for "failure" to bring a feeling of shame and ignite our inner critic. Although beating ourselves up may feel like a good idea at the time, it doesn't get us to achieve our goals.

Instead, be kind to yourself. This may look something like, "I didn't manage to achieve my goal this time, but that's OK. I worked really hard." Supporting your students to have this mindset can help them avoid procrastination and deep disappointment in themselves.

5. Tell your students to take breaks as needed

All of us must understand that we shouldn't sacrifice our sanity for the sake of our goals. Yes, completing your school work is important, but if a student is having a tough time staying productive and focused, it begs the question: "do you need a break?"

Taking a break, even a short one, can be hugely restorative. It can help give us a fresh mindset, allowing us to get the job done.

We've talked about all things planning, organization, and time management. Next on our to-do list is working memory. Anyone with classroom experience knows how painful it is to explain a set of instructions over and over again. It can exhaust even the best of us and leave us feeling more than frustrated. We may tell ourselves that our students aren't even listening. But the problem lies much deeper than this.

5

THE WORKING MEMORY

I don't know about you, but I feel like I use the biggest portion of my patience in the classroom. Question after question. Reminding students how to behave and repeating over and over again what they need to do. Don't get me wrong; I love my job. But it is exhausting. So, when I come home and ask my teenager to do something and then have to repeat it 2 minutes later, I'm pretty much ready to burst.

When we're tired and cranky, it's all too easy to assume that our students (and those who have children!) are doing this on purpose - deliberately trying to wind us up. But whenever I have thoughts like this, I remember working memory.

That's the topic of this chapter, and it's an important one, so stay tuned.

WHY IS OUR WORKING MEMORY IMPORTANT?

We've touched on what working memory is, but that was a fair few chapters ago, so let's refresh our minds and bring this information into our working memory!

Working memory is our temporary storage zone - where we hold information while doing other things. It's integral in our ability to:

- Comprehend information
- Reason
- Problem-solve
- Process and organize new information
- Connect new ideas with ones already stored in our brains
- Stay on task for long durations
- Control our automatic impulses
- Be flexible in our thinking
- Shift attention
- Apply different rules to various settings.

As you can see, working memory is crucial for every one of us. It's also interconnected with many other executive function skills, as you can see above. This means that struggling with working memory can cause a ripple effect across loads of other skills, too.

So, what are examples of everyday tasks we need working memory for? Well, we need working memory to remember things like phone numbers, where we've put stuff once we've set it down, and what we want to say in the middle of a conversation. Working memory is also essential for academic success, especially in literacy and numeracy.

Now, let's consider some general signs of struggling working memory.

SIGNS OUR WORKING MEMORY IS STRUGGLING

Let's run through some common signs that we may see if we're suffering from low working memory:

- Forgetting what you've read straight after reading it, so having to go back and reread it.
- Difficulty focusing your attention on any one thing for a long period of time.
- Many tasks seem to take you longer, particularly when the task involves processing new information.
- You may need to repeat something over and over again before you remember how to do it.
- Step-by-step instructions are challenging - this includes following a recipe, making flatpack furniture, or taking the trash out.
- It's a real struggle to remember people's names, even if you've met them more than once.

- It isn't easy to follow conversations because you may forget what the other person has said right after they said it or forget what you were going to say in response.
- You may constantly lose things because you can't remember where you set them down.
- People may ask, "were you listening to me?" because you agreed to do a task for them and then forgot to do it.

While some of these are general, a fair few relate more to adults than children. You may notice yourself, a friend or a family member do some (or all) of these things. Remember to be self-reflective if you notice these things about yourself; it's good to know if you're struggling with working memory, as this can impact your teaching.

But let's shift and focus on how working memory difficulties may arise in the classroom, as this is what this book is really about.

WHAT WORKING MEMORY LOOKS LIKE IN THE CLASSROOM

Roughly 70% of students with learning disabilities struggle with working memory. Low working memory is also common among children with ADHD. So, you'll definitely come across many students who find tasks requiring working memory challenging.

Children use working memory in 5 distinct ways: to assess information, remember instructions, pay attention, learn to read, and learn math. Let's take a look at each of these in turn.

1. Assess information

Auditory memory and visual-spatial memory are the two types of working memory. While auditory memory is responsible for taking in and processing what you hear, visual-spatial memory's job is to take a mental picture of what you see.

In this way, working memory is pretty similar to a video camera. Unfortunately, we can't play back this information whenever we want like you can on a video camera (as cool as that would be!). Instead, our working memory has to access and play back this information immediately, even when we're taking in new information to add to the existing information.

Think about a time when you've done number sequences in math. Your students need to keep all of the known numbers in their heads, try and solve the problem of what comes next, and then verbalize this or write it down. That's a whole lot of information to keep in your mind all at once!

This task is practically impossible for children with working memory difficulties. They can't remember the sequence of numbers you've told them about, let alone try and figure out what goes next in the sequence. It's like trying to solve a riddle when you only know half of it.

2. Remember instructions

You need to be able to combine existing knowledge with new information to do most activities in class, especially when you're following step-by-step instructions. This is super hard for children with working memory difficulties, as they struggle to combine both forms of information. They may struggle to remember what they've just done, which may mean they repeat the same step or get frustrated and quit.

3. Pay attention

Working memory and concentration are strongly connected because the same part of the brain is responsible for both. So, if a student struggles with working memory, more than likely, they will also find it challenging to stay on task for long durations.

When we're completing a task, our brain constantly reminds us of what the end goal is - what we're supposed to be doing. But kids with working memory difficulties may not remember the end goal, making the whole task seem pretty pointless. This may lead to them getting distracted and, more often than not, distracting most of their classmates, too!

4. Learn to read

When we're learning to read, auditory memory helps us remember the sounds of each letter of a word, which ultimately helps us to sound out the whole word. Visuospatial memory then allows us to store how words look so that we can remember them when we see them in the future.

This is another area where kids with low working memory suffer because they can't retain all of this information long enough to sound out the whole word. And if they do, they'll likely forget it by the time they come across the word again.

5. Learn math

Learning math is like building a house. You need lots of different layers of materials before you complete the construction. The very foundations of the house are our ability to recognize and reproduce information that forms patterns. Then, we add the first layer of bricks - using these patterns to remember and solve math problems.

Then, we keep adding bricks from there - we store information relating to a math problem and then utilize this information to help create our workings out.

The ability to remember, sequence, and visualize new information cements the whole house. Unfortunately, these skills are tricky for kids with low working memory.

Now, onto behaviors, you may see from children with low working memory in a classroom setting.

Working Memory-Related Classroom Behaviors

Children with working memory difficulties may show what we call "problem behaviors" - behaviors that disrupt their learning as well as the class as a whole. To clarify, the student is not the problem, the behavior is a result of a deeper issue. While these problem behaviors can be extremely frustrating for educators (trust me, I know!), it's important to remember that they're coming up because the child is struggling. This can help us to keep an empathic mindset.

Working Memory Related Behavior	Possible Intervention
The student requires multiple prompts to start or complete a piece of work.	Use concept maps to help the student bring multiple ideas together and form tangible connections between ideas. Go over what you learned about the topic previously to get old knowledge back into awareness.
The student struggles to "read between the lines."	Use concept maps to help the student bring multiple ideas together and form tangible connections between ideas. Go over what you learned about the topic previously to get old knowledge back into awareness.
The student finds it really challenging to remember a string of new information like a math equation, spelling, or vocab words.	Practice math facts - repetition can help them to process this information and transfer it into long-term memory. Try oral storytelling to help them string new bits of information together. Side-step fluffy language - if it's new information, brief and concise. Individualize memory aids.

Working Memory Related Behavior	Possible Intervention
The student frequently forgets or loses their belongings.	Teach them how to use checklists to ensure they come to class ready to learn. Adopt routines in class that help the student to check their belongings and return them to a specific place.
Once the student has remembered information, they find it challenging to apply it to other situations.	Give the student written step-by-step instructions using formula cards or by putting directions on the board. Model what you want them to do as well as tell them, and give them visual aids. Allow time for the student to repeat the task.
The student forgets or skips words, writes sentences that are too short, and displays low attention to detail.	Think about and eliminate external stimuli that are interfering with their working memory. Don't just tell them how to do something; show them. Use visual aids to help them process the information at their pace. Connect different concepts using concept maps and other visual tools.
The student forgets information they've just heard or read. They can't remember tasks they just agreed to and forget what they're about to say when speaking to you.	Use mnemonics and create visuals to help make information more memorable. Go over what you've learned a couple of times in the same lesson and then as an introduction in the next lesson. Simplify long processes into chunks so that the information is more digestible.

It's also good practice to listen in when speaking to parents about their children - what do they say about them? If parents report that their child is "lazy" or that they "don't really listen" and "need to be reminded all the time," then this suggests that 1) they're struggling with low working memory, and 2) this is affecting their home life.

If you have a conversation like this with a parent, you can start slipping in any of the interventions we've already gone through. You may be surprised by the difference they start to make!

The thing is, you will see improvements in your students by incorporating these interventions in response to their observable behaviors. But this is sort of like putting out fires as they arise; it's not dealing with the cause of the flames. In this way, responding to behaviors is a one-pronged approach. To see the biggest improvements in your students, you need to adopt a two-pronged approach, bringing in activities that will actively boost their working memory skills. Let's take a look at 7 key ways to do this.

7 WAYS TO BOOST WORKING MEMORY

Here, we take a look at seven ways to boost working memory. Of course, these aren't the only ones. But I will say that these are the seven methods I use the most because of how easy they are to implement in the classroom. They require only slight changes in technique, making our lives as educators much easier! So, what's number 1?

#1 Ask Students to Repeat Step-by-Steps Back to You

If there's one way to ensure students know what they're about to do, it's this. Once you've gone through the directions with a student, get them to repeat this to you. While this extra step may take a little bit of time out of your day, it won't take nearly as long as going back and telling them the next step every 5/10 minutes.

#2 Try Visualization Techniques

It can really help children with working memory difficulties to piece bits of information together in their minds so that it forms an interconnecting web. One way to do this is through visualization. If you encourage them to create a mental picture of all the information they need, this can help them to remember it. This technique works a lot like mnemonics.

#3 Give Clear, Concise Directions

Overloading a student with working memory difficulties with lots of information is a surefire way to make them forget the essential information. So, get rid of fluffy language and only tell the student exactly what they need to know. Keep your requests short and to the point, and break multi-step directions down, so they don't have to remember loads of things at once. Most importantly, post your directions (don't forget pictures for the non readers) so they can refer back and independently figure out what their job is.

#4 Teach Organization

We can't assume that our students will know how to organize themselves. We've got to take it upon ourselves as their educators to teach not only the educational content but all of the organizational components around this. Use concept maps and other visual aids to help them organize information in their mind, as well as systems to help them manage their belongings.

#5 Break Things Down

Write down precisely what the student needs to do so they have something to refer back to when completing a multi-step task. While this will take a little bit of preparation time, it will be worth it. You'll not only help your student be more independent, but you'll also improve their academic attainment!

#6 Praise, Praise, Praise!

Students with executive dysfunction get mostly negative feedback. This isn't great for their self-esteem or sense of self - they may see themselves as unable to do things, or they may even begin to believe that they're generally "bad." Giving them praise for their hard effort can significantly impact how they see themselves. I promise that picking out one thing the student has done well each day can make all the difference.

#7 Practice Note-Taking

We take for granted the difficulty of jotting down key information. You first have to remember all the information, then you have to sort through it to figure out what's the most important, and then you have to remember this to write it down. By the time a child with working memory difficulties has done that, they've missed other key information.

Get your child to write down their homework assignments and checklists to help them keep up with their work. Write down critical bits of information on the board, so they don't have to try to figure this out while you're teaching.

You can also use games to boost your students' working memory skills. Here are 5 fun games you can use in class to get your students working memory gears turning.

Remember 10 With Explorer Ben

This is a great working memory activity book that helps teach students different memory games with the help of explorer Ben. The book sections contain 10 things Ben needs to remember and ways to do it. Then, the student is shown some of the information, and the test is to identify the bits that are missing. This book is invaluable when it comes to encouraging independence.

Shopping List

This straightforward board game involves trying to find all the things on a shopping list. Other players will turn the cards another student needs over, and they have to remember where this is so they can return to it when it's their turn.

Scrabble

Many schools already have a scrabble set, so you may only need to ask around. Scrabble is really good for children who struggle to organize and plan, as it teaches them to strategize and combine existing and new information. It also works wonders when teaching vocab!

Distraction

Both you and your students will laugh at this one. Each player takes turns drawing number cards from the pack. They must remember the number sequence until one player draws the 'distraction card.' The person who draws the card has to answer a silly question and then say their number sequence in the order in which they drew their cards.

Simon Says

I'm not referring to the age-old game you can play to get kids to follow instructions, although this is also an excellent game to get students' attention and get them to refocus. However, the Simon Says I'm referring to is an electronic game that teaches students to remember patterns of colors that gradually get more and more complicated.

Hopefully, you've now got loads of helpful tricks and games to use when working with children with working memory difficulties. Let's move on to the next executive functions - flexible thinking and self-control.

Self-control is a fascinating one for me because it's something I've had to work on myself. I haven't ever had a raging temper that is out of my control, at least not at work, but I always struggled to adapt to change and solve problems that come with changing circumstances. With the COVID pandemic barely over, I know many parents and teachers have found this really challenging.

6

FLEXIBLE THINKING AND SELF-CONTROL

Did you know we have around 35,000 decisions to make every single day? Of course, most of these are simple, like choosing what to wear (although that can sometimes be challenging!). Others require our executive function skills. Without strong EF skills to help you, making so many decisions can be tiring. If we're not careful, things can quickly escalate from fatigue to mental burnout.

This next chapter hones in on preventing this emotional reaction (in ourselves *and* our students!). We will focus on how flexible thinking and self-control benefit students in a classroom and how we can help students to build upon their self-control skills.

ALL GOOD PLANS ALLOW FOR FLEXIBILITY

Children and adults with strong cognitive flexibility can change their approach to a task or problem if the method they're trying isn't working. They can also adapt to changes in their environment.

Allowing for flexibility in the classroom enables the teacher and students to adapt, see things from different perspectives, and come up with the best possible way to solve a problem.

But flexible thinking isn't just a skill for the classroom. Children need this skill for all manner of social situations, particularly when we face relationship problems, conflicts, and social conundrums.

For example, say you're a student about to finish your lunch break (preferred activity) and return to class (non-preferred activity). This could be a really tricky transition for someone with flexible thinking problems.

Other situations that may be challenging for people with low cognitive flexibility are:

- Trying a new method after one has failed.
- Changing your phrasing when someone doesn't understand what you're trying to communicate.
- Putting yourself in someone else's shoes and thinking about a situation from their perspective.

- Putting objects into categories, such as sorting them by color, shape, or function.
- Accepting that someone else's idea is more likely to work than yours.
- Being able to change what you're doing in the event of unexpected circumstances, such as when a child is supposed to go on a play date, but their friend is sick.

As you can imagine, a classroom looks very different with and without flexibility. Let's compare the two.

YOUR CLASSROOM WITH AND WITHOUT FLEXIBILITY

Each and every classroom needs flexible thinking to get by and achieve academic success. Without it, you'll likely see lots of "problem behaviors," including distraction, frustration, and refusal.

Consider this. One student really loves art, the first lesson of the day on Tuesdays. One Tuesday, they get stuck in a nasty traffic jam and miss half of the lesson. They finally get into school, and you can see that as soon as they walk into the door, they're frustrated - things haven't gone their way.

Someone with strong cognitive flexibility skills may see this as an unexpected annoyance but one that they couldn't predict, so they make the most of the time they have left in the lesson.

However, it may be hugely discombobulating for a child with executive dysfunction to not be present at the beginning of a lesson like they usually are. They may really struggle to engage in the rest of the lesson as a result. The change in their timetable may throw them entirely out of whack.

Other examples of a classroom without cognitive flexibility are:

- Students continually make the same mistake over and over again, driving you crazy!
- A student arguing the same point repeatedly with no let-up, even though you've tried patiently to tell them another perspective multiple times.
- Emotional outbursts, tantrums, meltdowns, and "problem behaviors" when rules and situations change unexpectedly.
- Dysregulation when you ask a student to change from one activity to another, especially from a preferred to a non-preferred activity.
- Getting frustrated over what seems like tiny changes to a routine.

A classroom with cognitive flexibility looks quite a bit different. Instead of the above, you will see:

- Students go with the flow, even when things don't go their way.

- Students demonstrating problem-solving skills - if plan A doesn't work, they automatically switch to plan B without prompts.
- Using real-life situations to compare and discuss things.
- You encourage activities that require perspective-taking, like students writing as if they're a character from a book.
- Teachers give their students a heads-up about upcoming changes to the timetable, like Sports Day.
- You practice coping strategies together to help de-escalate stressful situations.

Luckily, there are many fun ways to ensure your classroom displays the latter, not the former. Let's take a look at some of the options.

#1 Show Kids What Cognitive Rigidity Looks Like

Educating our students about any executive function will help them better understand themselves and their difficulties. It's no different with cognitive flexibility. You can get creative, giving fun, real-life scenarios of people showing rigid thinking.

Let's use an example. When given the question, "Find the difference between 8 and 6," a kid with cognitive flexibility may look at how the numbers look rather than the mathematical difference between them. The Research Institute for

Learning and Development showed this exact example - the student wrote, "eight is all curly, six is not" as a response (Research Institute for Learning and Development, n.d.).

You can also demonstrate cognitive flexibility to your students by showing them the question, "Name the quadrilateral," and then going ahead and giving each quadrilateral a human name. Your students will likely laugh at you for this, but it makes an important point.

#2 Crack a Cognitive Flexibility Joke

This technique is another excellent, funny way to bring in the topic of flexible thinking. Moreover, humor and quick wit help cognitive flexibility develop, so this technique is a double whammy.

Here are some good ones to try with your students:

- I've been telling everyone about the benefits of eating dried grapes. I've been raisin awareness.
- What can you say to a friend who's upset about their grammar? There, their, they're.
- I'm trying to organize a game of hide and seek, but I can't seem to find any good players.
- It's not wise to tell your clock all your secrets. Why, you ask? Well, only time will tell.

#3 Playing Games Differently

Encourage your students (and their parents!) to change the rules of the games they play. For example, they could slide down the ladders and travel up the chutes instead of the other way around. This may be tricky for them to get the hang of, to begin with, but soon enough, they'll find that they like changing the rules!

How does self-control tie into all of this?

THE BEAUTY OF SELF-CONTROL

You may have heard of the term "self-control" before reading it in this book, or you may have heard of "impulse control." They mean the same thing. The way I like to describe this executive function skill is "thinking before you act." That's what self-control is - it's all about a set of behaviors that stop us from acting on impulse, using more rational thinking to inform our decisions.

Have you ever heard a student say, "I need it now!", "I've got to do it!" or "I don't care, I'm doing it!"? This student likely had difficulties in self-control - they struggled to regulate their impulses and resist the urge to act automatically.

Self-control is an important executive function skill because children will need to learn how to control their negative behaviors as they age. While parents and educators will go out of their way to help a young child having a tantrum, we can't say the same for adolescents.

Self-control links with other EF skills, including planning, problem-solving, and flexible thinking. Without these skills, people may jump to the wrong conclusions, leading to adverse outcomes, and act on impulse.

Some common examples of scenarios that require self-control are:

- Turn-taking during conversations - speaking & then listening.
- Making your own decisions rather than giving in to peer pressure avoids unhealthy and even dangerous behaviors.
- Resisting the urge to talk back to a parent, teacher or, later in life, a manager.
- Persevering during a non-preferred, challenging task until you complete it.
- Stopping yourself from binging on food and knowing when to call it quits with spending and screen time.
- Sharing preferred activities and items, like snacks and toys.
- Prioritizing the most boring or challenging tasks.

So, how can you help students manage their impulses better?

HOW TO HELP STUDENTS WITH THEIR SELF-CONTROL SKILLS

We can help all of our students with their self-control skills - not one person's self-control skills are fixed. It just takes a little time and perseverance; that's all. Give some of these straightforward strategies a go to help your students better regulate their impulses.

#1 Create a Shared Journal

Have you ever come across a student keen to give their input in lessons? They always put their hand up to ask questions, pulling you aside wherever possible to share their thoughts with you. You don't want to discourage this behavior because this shows they're interested. However, it can be a bit of a pain in the middle of a lesson, as it can disrupt the flow, making it difficult for you to teach all your curriculum - and you're already on a tight schedule!

That's where a shared journal comes in. This is a journal that students can use to write their thoughts, questions, and connections relating to anything in class. You can allocate a time slot each day to go through the shared journal with this student, working through any questions they had and discussing their ideas. This is the perfect way to prevent constant interruptions in class while showing your students with self-control problems that you care and that their thoughts are valid.

#2 Use Social Stories & Picture Books

There's no need to talk about self-regulation directly - many children won't learn this way. Instead, why not try and implement this learning through picture books and social stories? There are some stellar books nowadays that really capture what it's like to struggle with self-control. Here are a few:

- Super George and the Invisible Shield - by Laurie Mendoza
- My Mouth is a Volcano - by Julia Cook
- Waiting is Not Easy! - by Mo Willems
- Lilly's Purple Plastic Purse - by Kevin Henkes
- We Don't Eat Our Classmates - by Ryan T. Higgins
- I'm in Charge of Me! - by David Parker
- What Were You Thinking? - by Brian Smith

You can also create your own social stories for your students. These give you a bit more flexibility as you can choose the character yourself - you may decide to pick their favorite superhero or cartoon character or even their favorite snack! The social story shows the main character facing a similar situation to the student - they are struggling with self-control. As the story progresses, your student will learn ways to regulate their impulses.

#3 Give Your Students Movement Breaks

No one likes being cooped up in a classroom for too long, least of all children with executive dysfunction. Giving your students movement breaks can help them get rid of excess energy. But what does this have to do with self-control? Well, by doing some physical activity, they're helping to regulate their bodies and, therefore, their impulses.

One trick I like is adding a movement or brain break after I've finished my instructions. You could get your students to run around the playground quickly, shoot some hoops, or even shake themselves and try to touch their toes in the classroom.

Always make your movement breaks different. Otherwise, children will lose interest in them and not want to engage. If they're fun, they'll get more out of it.

#4 Use Visual Reminders in Class

You can't beat visual reminders for helping children to remember to stay on task and do what's expected of them when they've gone rogue. You can place a visual reminder on a student's desk to remind them to put their hands up before answering questions, a reminder on the board showing the end-of-day routine and reminders by the door for when they have to wait in line.

#5 Get the Self-Control Games Out!

There are loads of games that encourage kids to practice self-control. For example, Simon Says. You can play this as a class to help them to refocus if they've become distracted, so this is a great one for sustained attention. But it's also massively beneficial for students who struggle with self-control, as they learn to resist the impulse to act on any instruction automatically. Another great game for self-control is Jenga. Jenga involves turn-taking, so students with self-control problems must practice waiting for their turn and resisting the urge to take the first piece they lay their eyes on.

More games that rely on self-control are: (You can find the rules by a quick search online)

- Sleeping Lions
- Guard Duty
- Blurt
- Freeze
- Wait Five
- Red Light, Green Light

You can also do things like mindfulness when the class becomes a little hectic and overly energetic in the classroom, discuss different real-life scenarios to brainstorm what self-control actually looks like in the real world, and role-play different situations like what a student would do if they had to wait in a queue. All of these tactics can make the difference for students struggling with self-control.

What's more, you can encourage your students to stop and think about a choice before they make it. You can support them through this by discussing the different possible outcomes. Give them coping strategies and develop some SMART goals together because the idea of being rewarded at the end will help them to get through the task.

We've covered all things self-control. Next on the agenda is perseverance. Like anything, more problems arise with perseverance when someone asks students to do something they don't want to do. And kids aren't the only ones that struggle with this. All you have to do is look at the ever-increasing piles of laundry and tax returns to know that we adults aren't all that different. But perseverance is essential - it's a crucial life skill. So, we've got to learn how to help students overcome difficulties with this EF skill.

7

PERSEVERANCE IN THE FACE OF CHALLENGES

> *"It's not that I'm so smart, it's just that I stay with problems longer."*

— ALBERT EINSTEIN

Einstein's quote says a lot about perseverance. If you haven't heard this one before, no doubt you've heard this: "if at first you don't succeed, try, try, and try again." Perseverance is something we need throughout life. You can't get by without it, and neither can our students, especially in an educational setting!

In this chapter, we'll persevere together, looking at why perseverance is an asset and how you can bring it into your classroom. We'll cover so many different methods, you'll definitely find something that suits your teaching style and class!

Let's get started.

WHEN THE GOING GETS TOUGH, THE TOUGH GETS GOING

Perseverance is an important quality for all of us to have. Without it, we face turning back at the first hurdle or staying down when we fall. If you think of anything important in your life, I bet you anything that you had to work for it - it didn't come just like that.

Consider your hobbies, relationships, and even getting up some mornings! If we didn't persevere in the face of challenges, we wouldn't get a whole lot done.

We can say the same for children. Our students need to be able to persevere for the same reason as us. Otherwise, they'll give up on complex tasks, their goals, and possibly their friendships.

Unfortunately, perseverance doesn't come as easily in today's world because of our "microwave culture." What do I mean by this? Well, we want everything done within a matter of minutes - waiting is out of the question. Think about all the new things children are exposed to now that you and I weren't during childhood - fast phone chargers, drive-throughs, next-day delivery, and even texting (depending on how old we are!).

How can we teach students to persevere in a world where they rarely need to wait for the things they want? The first step is understanding all of the benefits of perseverance ourselves so that we can educate our students on its importance. Here are 10 key motivations for being perseverant.

#1 Perseverance Helps Us Accept Failure

Many, if not all, of us aren't that comfortable with failure. I have always despised that feeling you get when you haven't succeeded at something. Failure is often deeply intertwined with shame, making it particularly tricky to bear.

But, if one thing's for sure, it's that we will all face failure at one point or another - it's inevitable. It can be much easier to cut your losses and quit when failure is on the horizon, but that doesn't get you anywhere in the long run.

Persevering in the face of potential failure helps you to realize that failure isn't the worst thing in the world. And you're certainly not a failure just because you didn't succeed at something. Perseverance helps us see that we're all learning and evolving - not one of us is perfect, and that's OK!

#2 Without Perseverance, You Can Say Goodbye To Your Goals

In the words of Theodore Roosevelt, "nothing worth having comes easy."

He wasn't wrong - any goal worth striving toward will take some perseverance on your part. Whether it's hitting the gym a couple of times a week or staying away from those complex carbs, we need perseverance to get us through.

Some goals will need more perseverance than others, granted. But all goals require the mindset to stick with them.

#3 Perseverance Is a Building Block to Success

It goes beyond perseverance helping us to overcome the fear of failure. The thing is, if you cop out and quit when things get tough, you are guaranteed to fail. But if you persevere, you've got a 50/50 chance of success.

Of course, more often than not, you're not going to succeed overnight. But, at least you have a chance when you persevere.

#4 Mental Health Flourishes From Perseverance

In their 18-year-long study, researchers Nur Hani Zainal and Michelle Newman found that goal persistence helps give people a sense of purpose, which in turn builds resilience

(American Psychological Association, 2019). From this resilience, we see a lower risk of depression, anxiety, and panic disorder.

So, perseverance isn't just good for our success and to lessen shame in the face of failure; it has real, tangible effects on our mental health.

#5 Perseverance Strengthens Relationships

We're social creatures. So for us, relationships are a fundamental part of life. Yet, they're not easy. Anyone who has been in a long-term romantic relationship *knows* there are trials and tribulations along the way. The key to keeping this relationship going is perseverance. With it, you'll build and grow together. Without it, the problems you can work through may lead to a relationship breakdown.

#6 We Won't Exercise Without Perseverance

I don't think there's a single adult in the universe who doesn't know about the benefits of exercise. We're encouraged to exercise everywhere - on social media, TV advertisements, and the news.

Yet, many of us still struggle to muster the motivation to exercise. One of the main reasons for this is that exercise can be challenging. So, regular exercise requires perseverance.

#7 Perseverance Helps Us To Learn

We adults aren't the only ones who face difficulties - our children (and students) face innumerable challenges. Their problems may not look identical to ours, but they're there. Difficult social interactions. A try for independence. Understanding who they are in the world. And on top of this, trying to learn.

If students choose to persevere, they open far more doors learning-wise. They get deeper into topics, gaining a broader understanding of the world.

#8 Perseverance and Adaptability Go Hand-in-Hand

We may not always reach our goals the way we envisioned. We may have to rethink our technique and change the method a handful of times. This is how perseverance and adaptability come hand in hand. Perseverance is all about adapting in the face of challenges. As we know, flexible thinking is a valuable EF skill, so perseverance's benefits are multifaceted.

#9 Those Who Persevere, Inspire

As an educator myself, I try to be someone who inspires others. One sure fire way to do this is to persevere when you come up against challenges.

Say you're having a pretty awful day at work; a change in the timetable has left your students unsettled and dysregulated. That's when your Smart Board decides to stop working. You're trying to get IT support, but it's just not panning out. You can respond to this situation in one of two ways:

1. **Give up.** Tell your students you can't teach the lesson and let them do a leisure activity.
2. **Persevere.** Model perseverance to your students by continuing with the lesson, even though you don't have the materials you thought you needed. You adapt in the moment and find a way to overcome the challenge.

Which response do you think would be more inspiring for your students?

#10 Perseverance Leads To Personal Development

We teach our students how to learn and develop all the time. When we have a second, most of us try to better ourselves, too. Perseverance helps us to grow and flourish as a person. Not only do we learn that we can do more than we thought we could, but we also gain knowledge and different perspectives along the way.

We figure out what we're really good at and what doesn't come naturally to us. And when things feel like they're against us, we learn how to muddle through.

As you can see, perseverance is pretty darn important. But how can we bring this essential skill into our classrooms?

WORKING IN A CLASSROOM WITH PERSEVERANCE

Riding a bike, practicing sports, giving a musical instrument a go - these things all require perseverance. If I tried to list everything we need perseverance for, I'd be here all day; neither of us wants that!

Perseverance is pretty easy to spot in students. They're typically the ones who have their head down and crack on. They work hard to better their scores and keep going even when things get tough.

Of course, there are fewer perseverant students. I'm sure you've come across a few in your career - those who get frustrated when they can't do something; or give up at the first signs of failure. Don't worry - there are 3 simple steps you can take to help these children out.

Step 1: Explain, Explain, Explain

The first step in bringing perseverance into your classroom is to teach your students what it actually is. I've already mentioned the importance of explaining concepts to students, but here I go again! I can't stress enough how vital it is to explain everything as you go because if you don't, you've lost your students from the start.

This doesn't have to look like a lecture. It doesn't have to be you standing up in the front talking endlessly about the importance of perseverance. You can make it into a group activity, letting your student brainstorm ideas on what they think persistence is, then you can come together as a class and discuss their thoughts.

You could even encourage them to create a concept map around perseverance. But again, explain what this is and model it for them!

Step 2: Be Your Students' Biggest Cheerleader

Praise is a powerful tool. Praising your students' effort, rather than their intelligence, can demonstrate to your students that they can achieve anything if they work hard enough for it. This is what we call a growth mindset. We mentioned this briefly earlier on, but let's recap. A growth mindset is when people believe their skills can improve with effort and practice. This is the polar opposite of a fixed mindset - the belief that our skills are fixed, that we have natural-born abilities that can't grow and develop.

Research demonstrates that 40% of students have a fixed mindset (Louick, n.d.). 40%! That's nearly half! Students with a fixed mindset struggle to find the motivation to work hard at something because they don't believe they can get any better. Because of this, they become stuck. This is one of the leading causes of procrastination and feelings of unfulfillment.

That's where praising effort rather than intelligence comes in. When you praise intelligence, you encourage students to have a fixed mindset. But when you commend their efforts, they learn they can do anything as long as they work hard and persevere.

One simple word makes all the difference for me - "yet." We often hear students say, "I can't do it!" or "I don't know how to do it!" I've learned to always finish their sentence with a "yet." This simple word shows them that I believe in them - I'm cheering them on.

Step 3: Show Acceptance of Mistakes

Creating a safe classroom environment is another biggie when teaching students to be perseverant. An environment that feels unsafe isn't conducive to learning for one, and it won't enable them to build upon their skills. Plus, we've already discussed the importance of a positive teacher-student relationship.

One of the best ways to strengthen your teacher-student relationships is to show acceptance of their mistakes. This can make the difference between them being unbelievably critical of themselves or accepting that they're only human.

You can even joke about it - telling your students that mistakes are your best teacher and that they make you look just about useless! The kids will love that. Give a little anecdote of a time when you made a mistake, and get your students to chip in with their own mistakes. This creates a space where it's safe to share.

You can also teach perseverance with games. More on that next! But first, here are some quick tools you can use to get your students to practice perseverance:

- Positive self-talk
- Brain breaks
- Be flexible - don't make them do anything you know will be unachievable, and allow them to get to the endpoint using their techniques if that helps
- Support them to set small goals
- Encourage them to ask for help
- Use checkpoints - you can make this fun by using a map with different locations and a 'prize' at the end
- Build breaks into achievement points

Now, bring on the games!

MAKING PERSEVERANCE A GAME

This section is jam-packed with fun games you can get your students to play. These activities naturally test their patience and perseverance, so they're great ones to incorporate into class time!

Game #1 Ping Pong Ball on Spoon Relay

This game can't be beaten for younger kids. Having to walk slowly to keep the Ping Pong ball on their spoon, then go back to the starting point if the ball drops to the floor. This is a classic game of patience and perseverance in the face of challenges.

But don't feel like you need to restrict this to only the younger years - you can change the difficulty of this activity using obstacles and changing up the size of the spoon or ball.

You can do this indoors or out, so it's the perfect test of perseverance!

Game #2 Bean Bag Toss

This is another game for all ages - for older students, you may want to move the 'goal' further away or get them to add a bounce. Encourage each student to set an achievable goal, like "I'll get three in a row."

Alternatively, you could get them to take basketball shots or play cornhole. There are so many different options, so get creative!

Game #3 Frog Hop

This is a fun little game involving frogs that 'jump' when you push them down on the table. This one may be more fun for younger kids, but consider your class! They may be up for it! Set up a little 'goal' for them and get them to make the frogs jump into the goal. Again, get them to set goals, so they're naturally more motivated to persevere. Remember to praise their efforts when they achieve their goal!

Game #4 Oreo Cookie Challenge

If your class isn't that into games, I'm sure they'll be excited about this! Get several different types of Oreos or similar brands. Then, tell your students to cover their eyes with a blindfold and yell out when they taste an original Oreo cookie.

You don't have to use cookies for this - it could be with fruit loops, different flavoured life savers, or anything that you can get different varieties of!

Game #5 Brain Teasers

Setting your kids a brain teaser a day can be a great way to start the learning before class even begins. Just put it on the board and encourage them to let you know when they think they've got it. Here are some brain teasers you can use:

People make me, save me, change me, and raise me. What am I?

ANSWER: Money

What five-letter word gets shorter when you add two letters to it?

ANSWER: Short

With pointed fangs, I sit and wait; with piercing force, I crunch out fate; grabbing victims with loads of might; physically joining with a single bit. What am I?

ANSWER: Stapler

Sally and George find some lettuce that has 20 leaves. Sally found the lettuce first, so she gets an extra leaf. How many leaves does Sally get?

10 ½ leaves

Seven sisters were born two years apart. The youngest sister is seven. How old is the older sister?

ANSWER: 19

What's the biggest number you can make with the numbers three, five, and seven?

ANSWER: 753

Game #6 Puzzles

Puzzles are the ultimate test of patience and perseverance because they take a while to complete. For example, a classic puzzle with around 1000 pieces will keep your students preoccupied for long periods of time because it'll take them a while to complete. You could make this simpler for younger students by using a puzzle with fewer pieces.

Another puzzle that tests perseverance is Sudoku. You can get your students to work together to complete this or let them work independently. Whoever completes it, in however long, will get a prize. This will encourage your students to keep going even if it takes a little while.

Game #7 Minute to Win It Stack Game

All you'll need to play 'Minute to Win It' is a blue cup and 8-12 red cups. Get your students to start stacking the cups into a pyramid with the blue cup on top. Then, direct them to continue until the blue cup is back on top. If their pyramid falls, get them to start from the beginning.

You can incentivize them by putting them in teams and getting them to race against each other or using a prize to motivate them.

Game #8 Ice Cream in a Bag

This isn't really a game, but it's so fun I just had to include it. You just need 5 ingredients for this easy recipe, making it awesome to do with kids of any age. You'll also need two Ziploc bags of different sizes - one big and one small. Get some half-and-half, salt, ice, vanilla, and sugar, and give your students a recipe to make their ice cream in a bag.

Make sure you support them through this task, as it won't be as easy for some kids to follow a recipe as it is for others. Remember, following step-by-step instructions requires strong working memory skills.

Here's a quick step-by-step that you can follow:

1. Fill the small Ziploc bag with 1 cup of half and half. Add 1 ½ teaspoon of vanilla and 1 tablespoon of sugar.
2. Seal the bag, getting all of the air out, then set the bag to one side.
3. Fill the big Ziploc bag ½ way with ice and add ¼ cup of salt.
4. Place your small Ziploc bag into the bigger one and continue to add ice until the big bag is full. Then, seal the larger bag.
5. Wearing gloves, shake the bag for 6 minutes.
6. Remove the small bag and rinse the outside of the bag. Be sure to rinse the seal; otherwise, you won't be able to get it open!
7. Open the small bag and mix with a spoon. Then, scoop out of the bag and enjoy!

The next skill set we will focus on is attention, also known as focus or concentration. For students to learn these skills, they need to follow the sequence. So, I don't recommend coming to this chapter until you've talked to your students about executive function - they need to master the language before learning about attention. They also need to have built on their working memory skills beforehand - this is pretty important because it'll be much harder for them to improve their attention if they're still struggling with their working memory!

But before all that, I've included a little handout you can use in class to help students accept their own mistakes. Enjoy!

WHOEVER HAS A MOUTH MAKES MISTAKES

Do you have a mouth?

If you answered "yes," and I really hope you did, then you make mistakes! And that's OK!

This phrase simply means that nobody's perfect - not one single person. We all make mistakes.

Mistakes help us to be more:

- Resilient!
- Knowledgeable!
- Creative!
- Human!
- Wise!
- Courageous!
- Understanding!

See, there are loads of things that mistakes help us with. But they can be hard to handle at first. And that's OK too! We'll all get there.

If you feel ashamed when you make a mistake, repeat this:

"Mistakes make me stronger."
"Mistakes make me wiser."
"Mistakes make me a human!"

And I bet you'll feel a whole lot better.

8

FOCUS AND ATTENTION

"Are you listening?"

"What did I just say?"

"Focus!"

"If only you'd pay attention."

It's shocking how many times, as a mother, wife, and teacher, I have said these phrases in the past. Before I knew about and fully understood executive dysfunction, I assumed that whenever a student was gazing out of the window or boinging their ruler off the end of their desk, they were purposefully *choosing* not to listen to me. And that made me frustrated, to say the least.

Now, I recognize that it's often the case that children really want to listen and pay attention, but they're unable to for long periods unless I support them to do so. If I put my energy into more effective methods, rather than wasting my breath on telling children with executive dysfunction to "Focus!" I can help them and myself!

WHAT GOES WRONG WHEN STUDENTS DON'T PAY ATTENTION

To learn, what does a student need to do? Turn up, for one, but that's a given. Once they've shown up to class, they need to focus. If they don't focus on what we're saying, they won't be able to learn new material or revise topics that we cover, and they won't have the foggiest idea about following instructions.

This information probably isn't new to you. But that's not all attention does. Attention is an essential executive function because it helps our students to tune out irrelevant information. Say their neighbor is clicking their pen while you're teaching a lesson. Instead of getting hooked on this distracting noise, someone with strong attention skills would be able to tune this out and solely focus on the learning material.

Picture attention like a sieve. All the distracting and unrelated information filters through, but the bigger, more important bits get stuck in the sieve.

Attention also gives students the ability to switch between conversations, which is super important if they're chatting to their neighbor and you call their name, telling them to sh. A child with attention difficulties may continue chatting away to their neighbor, utterly unaware that you're trying to get their attention. Whereas children with strong attention skills will likely hear their name immediately, and their attention will be diverted away from their conversation and towards you.

Then, there's attention's link to memory. If you're not focusing on what you're being taught, you're not going to remember it. When the information isn't even reaching your short-term memory, it will never land in your long-term memory; essentially, that potential learning is lost.

As you can imagine, students with attention difficulties are less likely to meet their potential in class. They may also get distracted and lose track of what they're doing, leaving a string of incomplete tasks in their wake. Students with attention dysfunction will miss important information and may even struggle to communicate with you and their classmates.

Attention difficulties are pretty common - and typically more severe - in students with processing problems, ADHD, and learning disabilities. Of course, not all kids with a condition will have attention difficulties. And some kids without one of these conditions will have attention difficulties, too. So, it would help if you learned how to spot when a class is focused - more on that next.

HOW TO SPOT INATTENTIVE STUDENTS

There are some signs of inattention that all of us can see. For example, have you ever had a daydreamer in your class who spends the day staring out of the window, not listening to a word you say? If you have experience with a student like this, you know very well when they aren't paying attention to you!

But there are other, more subtle signs of inattention. Let's take a look at some:

- **Communication issues:** children with attention dysfunction typically show poorer communication skills because they can't concentrate on a conversation for long periods. They may 'zone out' mid-way through a conversation, forget the topic of conversation, or struggle to ignore distractions.
- **Forget important information:** you may make it explicitly clear to your students what parts of a topic are the most important. But if they aren't focused during the few seconds you tell them it's essential, they won't ever remember it.
- **Task flip-flopping:** the student may move between tasks abruptly without completing the first one. For example, a student with attention difficulties may go to pick up a sharpener, put their pencil down while they're looking for it, then take the sharpener back to their desk and forget where they put their pencil.

You may also notice attention dysfunction if you call on a student to answer a question only to realize they have absolutely no idea what you are saying. Or, maybe you've noticed a student go to an area of your classroom with a purpose but completely forget what they went there for when they get there.

Whatever the sign of attention difficulties, we as educators need to do something about it to help our students learn. So, what can we do?

TRICKS TO GET YOUR STUDENTS' ATTENTION (AND KEEP IT!)

There are all kinds of tricks to get your students to pay attention. You can try either getting their focus in class when their mind has wandered or playing games that strengthen their attention skills. I recommend a combination of both for the best results!

Befriend Your Students' Parents

One tip I always recommend to teachers attempting to help their students with attentional difficulties is to get to know their parents. While this doesn't always sound necessary for every single child, for children with attentional dysfunction, it's vital.

Why is this? Because parents know their children better than anyone. So, we're missing a trick (and valuable information!)

if we're not building strong relationships with our student's parents. Working collaboratively with parents helps to maximize the support measures in place for the children - both academic and pastoral.

You can build relationships with parents in various ways:

- Share success stories
- Convey empathy towards the parents when speaking to them by listening, not responding with judgment, and validating their concerns.
- Start early - it's never too early to build relationships with your student's parents. Start as soon as you become their child's teacher.

Grab Students' Interest With Games

If you've ever played games with your students (maybe you've even tried some from earlier in the book!), you'll know that students gobble games up like they're eating their first meal in a week - they love the opportunity to play something fun and interactive.

You can incorporate short games into your teaching to bring your students' focus back into the room if distractions lead it astray. Try one or more of these:

- Simon Says
- Distraction
- Radar Focus

- I Spy
- Keep the Story Going
- Zap!

Having some physical games in your classroom is also great for helping your students practice sustained attention. Some of the best ones I'm aware of are the Elephant Stampede safari adventure game, Chess, Scrabble, Go, and Quarto.

Going off on a slightly different idea, you could try regular mindfulness activities or sleeping lions. Sleeping Lions is especially good if your students struggle with hyperactivity, too - you get them to lay on the ground and stay as still as they can as if they're sleeping lions. If they move, they're out. The last person to be called out wins.

Those are two of the main tricks I use to get my students' attention. But here are some other techniques that I know work a treat:

- **Preferential seating:** Seat children who struggle with attention at the front of the classroom, with exposure to fewer distractions, and far away from windows. Keeping them closer to you will also help you to prompt them if they become distracted.
- **Shorten tasks:** When planning your lessons, remind yourself to keep tasks short and snappy so you don't disadvantage the inattentive kids. Alternatively, get a kitchen timer and set it on the student's desk if you

can't shorten the task. When it goes off, your student knows it's time for them to check in with you about their progress.

- **Clear the desks:** Cluttered desks are responsible for distraction a lot of the time, so encourage your students to clear their desks of clutter as often as possible.

- **Set a single task:** If you know you're going to be asking your students to complete multiple tasks, set the students with attentional difficulties just one at a time. If this means cutting up the worksheet and giving them out one after the other, do it! Trust me; it's worth it!

- **Make eye contact:** Eye contact is a powerful motivator to stay focused. If you're walking a student through a set-by-step, keep eye contact as much as possible. They may avoid it at first, but they'll get used to it and become more comfortable.

- **State expectations clearly**: Use verbal, pictorial *and* written guidance to help your students fully understand what you expect of them. This teaches them to be more independent and know where to look when they need those all-important reminders.

Next, we're onto the penultimate chapter of this book. In Chapter 9, we focus on how to support your students to get started on tasks straight away. While prompts and cues from you will form a big part of this, to begin with, the ultimate aim is independence, so that's the second part of the chapter.

But just before that, here's a useful little handout showing the average concentration time for students of different ages. This can be helpful, so your expectations aren't unrealistically high!

How Long Can I Focus?

Our attention gets better as we get older. By the time we're 20, 30, or even 60, the part of our brain responsible for attention has had lots of practice. This means that the attention spans of young children who haven't been able to exercise this muscle as much are likely to be much, much shorter than adolescents and adults.

Age	Average Attention Span
2 years old	4 - 6 minutes
4 years old	8 - 12 minutes
6 years old	12 - 18 minutes
8 years old	16 - 24 minutes
10 years old	20 - 30 minutes
12 years old	24 - 36 minutes
14 years old	28 - 42 minutes
16 years old	32 - 48 minutes

If we think about it this way, school tests kids' attention spans to their very limits. And these figures are for neurotypical children who don't have executive dysfunction difficulties.

For kids with ADHD, learning disabilities, and other conditions affecting attention, these timeframes will be a whole lot lower. This is worth keeping in mind while you're planning your activities - don't overload your students because those with EF difficulties won't stand a chance.

9

TASK INITIATION AND INDEPENDENCE

It's one thing to explain an activity to a child so that they understand it. It's a-whole-nother thing for them to get on with it independently. If students with executive dysfunction haven't tripped at the hurdle of paying attention, they'll likely stumble when it comes to starting the task without continual prompts or further guidance.

Looking back on my experience as a mother, my children's earliest stages of independence and wanting to do things on their own was when they were toddlers. This seems early but think about it. They run riot as soon as they get the chance - sometimes from as early as 10 months. They also want to do things independently, like eating, painting, cutting, etc.

The problem I faced was that those actions terrified me - I was so worried about them hurting themselves when they started walking. Then, when they were old enough to clutch a pair of scissors and eat by themselves, I took the scissors away from them or fed them with my more nimble handles.

Even when they're teens, we often do things for them because we think they'll do it wrong, or the need for constant nagging instills the idea that they won't ever do it at all!

Unfortunately, as time passed, I realized how limiting this was to their independence. Every time I did something for them, I was 1) reinforcing the idea that they can't do it themselves and 2) not allowing them to learn.

Hindsight is a wonderful thing.

In this chapter, we talk about terminology and explore what task initiation and analysis paralysis are. Then, we think about how you can spot the signs of independence in your class and ways for you to encourage independence.

WHAT'S TASK INITIATION?

Completing any task, whether it's their absolute favorite thing to do or something they hate, requires a whole load of executive function skills, including:

- Planning
- Prioritizing
- Time management

- Organization
- Impulse control
- Attention
- Working memory

You can see how completing a task may be challenging for someone with executive dysfunction, especially if those difficulties are severe. However, the most detrimental problem is often the inability to get started on a task. Without starting the task, you most definitely won't be finishing it!

The term we use for 'starting a task' is task initiation. This is a fundamental EF skill that all students need to learn. Task initiation is much more than just getting started - we will all come across things we *must* do at some point. The real key to task initiation is beginning the task *on time.* That means no procrastination. That's the sticking point for most students I've taught over the years.

Here are some everyday tasks that children with task initiation difficulties may struggle to start:

- Tidying their room
- Completing their homework
- Cooking dinner
- Starting a task in class
- Getting ready

When our students struggle to start a task, we attentive educators are typically quick to offer our assistance. We may do this through a prompt, crouch down and offer some 'helpful' guidance, or pick up their pen and start going through it with them. But what does this do? It takes away their independence.

Independence benefits children in many ways. It gives them:

- More confidence
- More control over their life
- A sense of importance
- Self-awareness
- Self-motivation
- An ability to make decisions effectively
- The opportunity to develop other qualities.

Independent children also tend to be happier and healthier because they are in the driver's seat in their own lives - they rely on themselves, not others, to get where they need to go. And as teachers, we need to be encouraging this mindset. Not just for the sake of our students but also for our sanity as teachers. After all, if we had a class full of dependent students, we wouldn't get a lot done in a day, would we?

ANALYSIS PARALYSIS: WHAT IT MEANS FOR STUDENTS

Analysis paralysis sounds pretty complex, but don't worry. It's an easy-enough concept - it's a type of procrastination where the person experiences overwhelm. Analysis paralysis differs from your regular, run-of-the-mill procrastination. Instead of dreading the task, you're so overwhelmed by the following:

a) the number of choices
b) the prospect of making a mistake
c) a potentially negative outcome

Because of this, you don't start the thing at all. Or, you severely delay starting, at least.

I'll set it out for you using an example. You're going out for dinner with your partner. They ask you where you want to eat, and you hesitate. You think, "this should be an easy enough decision." Yet, the pressure of the decision sets in, and you think, "what if I make the wrong choice?", "what if I hate the food I'm eating?" and "what if my partner doesn't want XYZ?"

The bombardment of questions in your mind quickly becomes overwhelming. The "simple" decision becomes too much to bear.

This scenario may not be realistic for you or me - we may just choose where we want to eat and skip the anxiety part. But this situation is possible for those who struggle to compare and consider several options, like some people with learning disabilities or ADHD.

You see, making a decision involves:

1. Starting the task
2. Paying attention to all the essential information
3. Remembering the details of everything so you can compare them
4. Considering different options
5. Acknowledging the pros and cons of each option
6. Analyzing the potential consequences of a decision.

Put that way, you can see how someone may struggle, particularly if they have working memory, cognitive flexibility, or problem-solving challenges.

Let's bring this back to the classroom. What are some things you can look for in your students? There are some characteristic signs of analysis paralysis:

- A student becomes frustrated when it's time to initiate a task.
- Putting their head in their hands or their head down when you instruct them to work independently.

- A student repeats, "I don't know what to do," when you've just explained exactly how to do it. This may even be the case if you've broken it down.
- Doodling instead of working on a task independently.
- A student who always finds something else to do instead of getting on with their work. This could be getting another pen, sharpening their pencil, going to the bathroom, getting a drink, etc.

It's important to remember that, although this behavior is frustrating for us teachers, our students aren't doing it intentionally to upset us. This may be something that they're really struggling with, but they have no idea how to explain it.

Patience is crucial in these situations. And so is having the right tools in your toolkit! We'll come to that soon. But first, how can you tell a class is independent?

SIGNS INDICATING YOUR CLASS IS INDEPENDENT

Just like some signs suggest the students in your class aren't dependent on you, there are things to look out for that indicate your students are independent. These could be when your students:

- Start the assignment straight away.

- Take the initiative to complete a task without being prompted and reminded to do it.
- Follow daily routines without being told.
- Set a timer or countdown to start.
- Exercise or use body breaks before starting a task.
- Create a daily schedule that they have practiced to the point of rote learning.

But just like with everything else with executive functioning, we can't expect our students to know how to do all of this from the off-set. We need to model all these behaviors and show them how to use the helpful tools to set them on the path to success.

HOW TO KEEP YOUR STUDENTS FOCUSED AND INDEPENDENT

I could go on all day about tasks you can use to keep your students focused *and* independent. But, for your sake, I won't do that. Instead, I've gone into detail about four of my favorite techniques and listed some of the others you can try!

Escape Room Style

If you have a set of assignments that you think may be tricky for some students to complete, make it into a game. One of my favorite methods is making the assignments seem like an escape room - each task is a clue that helps them escape the room.

The only thing to consider in this scenario is that kids may get highly competitive and want to do it as quickly as possible. While that's great, if they're not doing their work as best they can, this won't help them learn. Ensure you remind them that the quality of their work still has to be high.

Buddy Up

Pairing students in 'buddies' can be an excellent way for your students to be more independent and start the task on time. This trick has always worked wonders for me because it gives your students the independence to get started without your aid but still with a little helpful nudge from someone. It can also be an excellent way for students to bond and form new friendships, which can be challenging for some kids with executive dysfunction.

Play Countdown

There's no reason why you can't make starting a task a kind of game. I like to put a countdown timer on in the interim between teaching and beginning a task. Kids will often rush around getting all the bits and bobs they need, then be ready and sit down for when it's time to actually get started.

This beats you constantly telling them to hurry up or prompting them to get started. If an automated timer can do it for you, that's a win-win in my eyes!

Allow Breathing Space

Allowing students to start new tasks can be anxiety-provoking and time-consuming; it's often easier to take the thing off them and do it ourselves. For example, if a student is trying to figure out a math question, but you need to move on to the next question because the rest of the class has already finished, you may grab the student's pen and quickly talk them through how to work the answer out.

While this can seem like the right thing to do at the moment (after all, it gets the job done, doesn't it?), this encourages dependence, not independence. If the student needs you every time they answer a math question, you will keep having this difficulty.

Therefore, allowing breathing space and flexibility in your teaching makes you feel less under pressure, giving your students the time they need to do their work themselves. Yes, they may need a little help from you, but ultimately, they must do the task.

Additional Techniques to Try

Here are some more that you can use to keep your student's focus while encouraging independence:

- Use fidget toys for hyperactive children - this can keep their energy levels down and make them less likely to get distracted.

- Give students with executive dysfunction every other question to complete.
- Set a schedule for them to clean and tidy their workspace.
- Reduce the demand on students with executive dysfunction in tasks you know they struggle with.
- Start by taking turns writing sentences.
- Show your students how to take brain breaks.
- Teach them about what task initiation is and what the signs are.
- Give them choices - rather than giving them one question that they have to answer, provide them with the choice of two or three.
- Give instructions in writing as well as orally.
- Show your students how to create a daily checklist.

You're almost at the end - we have one chapter left. There's been a lot of learning in these 9 chapters so far. In this last chapter, chapter 10, we'll bring it back to you - what your own EF strengths and weaknesses are and how you can self-reflect in order to learn and improve in the future. Are you ready?

SELF-REFLECTION AND METACOGNITION

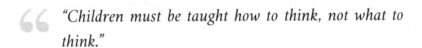 *"Children must be taught how to think, not what to think."*

— *MARGARET MEAD*

Our main job as educators is to teach. That may seem obvious, but what we need to teach is more than just the curriculum. The impact we have on our students can either be minuscule or massive.

To have a massive impact, we need to teach them past the curriculum by giving them lessons on the skills we've explored in this book. The final piece of the puzzle is teaching self-reflection and metacognition, so they know not just to think but to understand and be aware of their whole thought process.

This chapter focuses on what metacognition means, what it does and doesn't look like, and how you can incorporate it in your classroom using different methods.

WHAT DOES 'METACOGNITION' MEAN?

An executive function coach, Seth Perler, describes metacognition as "understanding of one's thought life and emotional needs."

In simple terms, metacognition (also known as self-reflection) is what we know about our thoughts - our awareness and regulation of our cognitive processes. This type of thinking is deeper than our everyday thoughts - for example, it's one thing to think, "I want a burger," and another to think, "I'm thinking a lot about wanting a burger right now because I haven't eaten lunch today."

Effectively, you're exercising your metacognition every time you stop and think about a particular thought in more depth.

We use metacognition for various reasons, but one of the primary purposes is to help us reflect on our past experiences. It allows us to notice things that work (or don't!) and keep them consistent or change things up. There are also some teacher-specific benefits of self-reflection:

- It helps us with our professional development
- It creates a student-centered learning environment
- It increases our self-confidence in our strengths

- It encourages us to be honest with ourselves and our students
- It keeps the lessons current as we are constantly learning and evolving

Metacognition is all about being conscious of what we're doing and how we're thinking and feeling. It's about being aware of the task we're working on and analyzing whether we should do it differently or similarly in the future. How, as educators, can we make our lessons more: fun, engaging, informative, and up-to-date?

To figure that out, we need to explore what metacognition looks like in a classroom setting.

WHAT METACOGNITION LOOKS LIKE

Seth Perler suggests one way to show metacognition is to **'Think Aloud.'** This simply means to think aloud about the activity you're doing. You can model metacognition using the 'Think Aloud' approach in several ways.

For example, while firing up your laptop and getting your students' resources ready, you could say, "I'm just thinking about how you're all sitting so patiently waiting for the lesson to begin, and I'm really grateful that you're being so attentive to your learning."

Beginning to bring this into your teaching can profoundly affect your students' metacognitive abilities, as they are likely to naturally mimic what you're doing, either verbally or in their head.

What's excellent about Seth Perler's approach is that you can do this anywhere. You could be walking and thinking to yourself, "Wow, I'm walking, and I'm thinking about the fact that I'm walking and how amazing it is to be able to move my body like this."

Or, if your students are reading, they could think, "Every day, I do reading, and I'm doing it right now. Although it doesn't look like I'm doing much, I'm reading."

That's just one way students may demonstrate metacognition in your classroom. Here are some other things they can try to exercise their self-reflection:

- **Deciding what material to study for a test**, e.g. "this material doesn't seem like it relates to the test as much as this does, so I'm going to choose to study this material."
- **After completing a piece of work**, e.g. "I think I rushed that last part; it shows in my writing. It looks like I haven't thought it through as much."
- **Checking through their work before handing it in**, e.g. "There is a spelling error which I need to sort out, and I could word that sentence better. I could also rephrase that and add some more detail here."
- **Study notes before assessments**, e.g. Review sheets

You can also do several things to bring out your students' metacognitive side. For example, you can make time for your students to redo their work. You could do this by 1) asking your students what they think they did wrong and 2) allowing them to fix any mistakes.

You can also dust off those KWL exercises from many moons ago. If you're not familiar with these, KWL stands for:

1. **Know about a topic:** you give your students a KWL chart and allow them to write down everything they know about a topic.
2. **Want to know:** chat with your students about what they want to know about a topic, writing down any questions they have in the W column.
3. **Learned in the end:** the final task of the lesson can be for students to fill out what they now know about the topic after the class. They can answer all of the questions they have written, and if there are still some unanswered questions, you can give them the opportunity to ask them.

For example, I would start the "weather unit" with a title page. My students can then put all they know on it. At the end of the unit, they add to the title page - this is a form of self-reflection that helps them see how much they learned.

So, if that's what metacognition looks like, what *doesn't* it look like?

WHAT METACOGNITION DOESN'T LOOK LIKE

Metacognition is relatively easy to spot in a classroom when you know what you're looking for. This also means it's glaringly apparent when a class doesn't have strong metacognition skills.

Let's take a look at some of the ways this becomes apparent.

#1 Poor Problem-Solving

For starters, students will have poor problem-solving abilities. Metacognition helps us to be more resilient when facing challenges. So, if students haven't had enough practice at metacognition, they may struggle with math problems or when you set them a task that they don't immediately know how to do.

Whereas a metacognitive student could ask themselves, "why am I getting stuck on this math problem?", "What is frustrating me?" and "what can I do to succeed?".

#2 The Learning Gap Gets Bigger

Kids with learning disabilities must work much harder to maintain the same learning standard as neurotypical students. When they also struggle to self-reflect, they fall even further behind.

A student who has had practice at self-reflecting would be able to consider why a task is frustrating and use this as a way to find a solution. Perhaps their first method isn't working, so they need to adapt.

Whereas kids who aren't as familiar with self-reflection will likely get stuck in the frustration stage, not knowing where to go. This makes it much harder for them to learn at the same pace.

#3 'Uncontrollable' Emotions

Metacognition helps us to regulate our emotions, so if we don't have that, our feelings will likely be all over the place. It's our dream as educators to see our students engage in self-regulated learning.

If you're unfamiliar with the term, it simply means they can work towards their goals. They may face hiccups along the way, such as frustration, wrong methods, and other roadblocks, but they can get past them on their own, with minimal support, to continue progressing.

Unfortunately, it's much harder for those without metacognitive strategies to reach their goals because they aren't able to think about what's going well, what's not, and how to overcome the roadblocks.

#4 Fixed Mindset

The whole point of metacognition is that we can grow based on self-reflection - if we notice that something isn't working how we want it to, we can shift our perspective and change our methods to grow and succeed.

When we can't self-reflect, we assume that the talents we are born with are the only talents we will ever have. We miss the opportunity to evolve and progress because we limit our capabilities.

#5 Unengaged and Inactive

Students who haven't had enough practice at metacognition often become inactive and unengaged learners for all the reasons listed above. And it makes sense, really.

If you believe that your capabilities are fixed, you can't control your emotions, you're way behind your classmates in learning, and you get stuck when you face a problem, why would you want to keep working hard? I know that I wouldn't.

So, we must help our students to boost their metacognition in any way we can. Next, we'll go through some games and handy techniques to promote metacognition in your students!

PROMOTING METACOGNITION WITH GAMES & OTHER HANDY TECHNIQUES

Let's start with three practical techniques you can implement in your lessons, then finish with the fun stuff.

3 Practical Techniques

#1 You, Plan, Do, and Review

This technique is all about creating a lesson structure that embeds metacognition right in. Let me break this down:

- **YOU:** As a starter exercise, ask your students to write down all the information they know about a topic and strategies they have used to help them learn the topic.
- **PLAN:** In this stage, you set your students a learning goal. It's their task to plan how they will achieve this goal, including their chosen strategies and timeline. They also need to consider what hurdles they may face.
- **DO:** This is where your students get to work - they follow their plan and attempt to meet the learning goal you have set for them. It's important that they review their progress during the doing stage, so stop the activity halfway and ask them to reflect on how things are going. If things aren't going so well, give

them some time to brainstorm a potential solution, then start the clock again.

- **REVIEW:** The review stage is an opportunity for your students to review what they have learned throughout the task. Did they meet the learning goal? Did they stick to their plan? Did everything in their plan work, or did they have to change their tactics?

Building this into your lessons will give your students a chance to practice metacognition, and they will likely not even know you're doing it, so you don't need to get bogged down in the detail of explaining what metacognition is!

#2 Traffic Lights

I love the traffic light system, not solely because it encourages students to reflect on their lessons but also because it helps me see where they're at.

You can use a traffic light system within your classes to make it easy for your students to let you know what they find challenging. Red could signify the parts of the lesson they didn't understand, amber to communicate the bits they found thought-provoking and green the aspects they understood well.

This encourages them to think about their knowledge and understanding of a topic, naturally exercising their metacognition.

This technique is perfect for primary-aged children because this age group will struggle to review their work or discuss metacognition with you.

#3 Balance the Scales of Difficulty

Giving students who struggle to learn topics easier work can be tempting. You want to help build their confidence so that they can tackle more challenging tasks in the future. While this may have some benefits, it doesn't help them in the long run.

Challenging work is more memorable. Your students aren't going to remember breezing through a math paper, but they will recall if they struggled but overcame this problem.

Challenging your students also means exercising their metacognition. They will have to reflect on the fact that their initial method isn't working and figure out an alternative way to solve the problem.

But, as educators, it's our responsibility to balance the scales of difficulty. Yes, we need to give them a task that challenges them, but we don't want to completely kill our students' confidence by setting up a task that's way out of their capabilities.

We've got to find the happy medium - something we know is within their grasp but will still be tricky for them to accomplish.

3 Metacognitive Games

#1 Blurt

Blurt includes a set of cards with definitions for different vocab words. Either you or a designated leader reads the card, and your students "blurt" out the answer.

You can do this as a class, but this can quickly become chaotic. Instead, I like to invite two students to battle against each other. While other students are present, it's their responsibility to keep quiet and only allow the two students who have been chosen to blurt out the answer. This is also a great test of self-control!

#2 Ball Pass

This is an activity to do as a whole class. The facilitator (most often you, the educator) holds the ball and asks a question. Any students who know the answer will raise their hand. You will throw the ball to one of the students with their hand raised, and they will answer the question. They then add their contribution and pass the ball on.

#3 Fish Bowl

Again, this is an activity for the whole class. To set up the space for this activity, create an inner circle using 3-4 chairs and an outer circle with all remaining chairs until there's enough for everyone to have a seat. Choose students to sit in the inner circle, then allow the others to sit in the outer ring. If students are reluctant to be in the inner circle, reassure them that they will be able to join the outer circle in a second!

Next, ask a question. Students in the inner circle can leave if they choose to, and others can take their place and join the discussion.

MY TIME TO SHINE

There is always a never-ending list of things to do when your students leave for the day. First order of business, a deep sigh of relief that you got through the day! Then, it's time to clear up, pack things away, pick stuff off the floor, and prepare yourself for tomorrow.

But, if at all possible, dedicate 5 - 10 minutes to yourself each day for your self-reflection. And, if you want to get the absolute most out of your self-reflection, do this with your planning. Think about what worked well today, what could see some improvement, and how you will make that happen.

Ask yourself, "what did I learn about my students today?" and "how can I use this knowledge to help them become better learners?"

You do this, and I guarantee you'll see improvements in your performance and your students' in no time.

CONCLUSION

Executive function skills are a fundamental aspect of life. Like air traffic control averts plane crashes, our executive function skills prevent our brains from crashing. Without them, we don't stand a chance.

We can't stick to deadlines and follow step-by-step instructions without **planning, organization,** and **time management.** Without **working memory,** we can't keep information in our heads long enough to use it for problem-solving. When we're unable to **think flexibly,** we become overwhelmed and unregulated when we face unpredictable changes.

Getting started on a task without procrastination is near-impossible without skills in **task initiation,** and paying attention long enough to learn is out of the question with a short **attention** span.

Maybe we have all these skills to a certain degree, but if we lack **perseverance** and **self-reflection**, we will stumble at the first hurdle, quit while we're ahead, and fail to learn from our mistakes.

As you can see, there's not one executive function skill we can live without. However, we're yet to mention the most devastating disadvantage of all. **Without EF, we're incapable of learning.**

Fortunately, we all have some EF skills to some degree. However, many students struggle with these, especially those with ADHD or learning disabilities.

As educators, we must be aware of the different executive function skills and the impact of executive dysfunction on our student's learning. If we're not, we risk giving some students an unfair advantage, leaving some kids trailing behind. I know none of us want that - we want to help each student reach their full potential, especially those that struggle.

Moreover, we want to appreciate each student on their own merits. When we're bogged down in the weight of time pressure, deadlines, and a whole curriculum to teach, it's easy to forget that the students who are playing up, acting out, or daydreaming their lives away, are struggling. Rather than internally rolling our eyes or telling them to "focus" again and again, we need to help them to thrive by bringing in techniques that develop their EF skills to the entire class so it reaches EVERYONE.

When we embrace our students' differences and recognize their EF difficulties, we become better teachers, and our students become better learners. I know this because I have experienced it myself. I know what it's like to dread the beginning of the year - to feel completely overwhelmed by the wealth of different skills, behaviors, and personalities your students display.

But now that I have all of the EF tools in my toolkit and know how to bring EF activities into my lessons seamlessly, I embrace these initial days, getting to know each student individually and thinking about the impact I can make on their lives.

And we can achieve all this in three simple steps. Step one is recognizing that there is a gap in our curriculum, that students aren't able to learn because their EF skills are holding them back. Learning the tools you need to do something about it is step two. The third and final step is bringing the techniques into your lessons so that everyone can benefit as a win-win!

You realize there's a problem. Otherwise, you wouldn't be here. Together, we've gone through tips and tricks you can implement in your lessons. Now, the ball's in your court. Go and knock it out of the park.

LIKE WHAT YOU SEE?

I love hearing about how other teachers and educators like yourself are making a difference in children's and young people's lives. If you liked (or even loved!) what you have seen in this book, please leave a quick Amazon review. This will encourage other nervous and struggling teachers to access the same advice, implement the same techniques, and make the same impact on their students' learning. Thanks so much for reading!

If you'd like to contact me you can go to my website **executivefunctioning.ca** and send me an email. I'd love to hear from you.

You can view the *self assessments* on the following pages or else scan the QR code for easier printing access! Enjoy!!

Name: _____ Date: _____

Planning
Having a plan to achieve a goal.

Check the boxes that are true for you	often	Sometimes	Rarely
I like to make list			
Sometimes I end up doing more work than necessary because i didn't think it through.			
I use agendas/calendars effectively.			
I have my things ready for the next class.			
I prioritize tasks in order of importance.			

For each check in sometimes or often complete the following

I need to do less of...

I need to do more of...

I learned that i'm good at

Name: _____ Date: _____

Executive Function Skills

Organization
Keeping track of your belonging & plans

Check the boxes that are true for you	often	Sometimes	Rarely
I often forget things either at school, home or going to places			
My room and desk are not neat & tidy.			
I tend to lose things.			
I don't finish tasks or assignments.			
I priortize tasks in order of importance.			

For each check in sometimes or often complete the following

I need to do less of...   I need to do more of...

I learned that I'm good at

Name: _____ Date:_____

Executive Function Skills

Time Management
Getting Things done in a timely manner.

Check the boxes that are true for you	often	Sometimes	Rarely
I easily get distracted and don't always start tasks right away.			
My work or task usually done late.			
I misjudge how long something might take.			
I put things off and start last minute.			
I can tell time on an analog clock.			

For each check in sometimes or often complete the following

I need to do less of...   I need to do more of...

I learned that I'm good at

Name: _____ Date: _____

Working Memory
Holding onto information

Check the boxes that are true for you

	often	Sometimes	Rarely
I can remember details.			
I need information repeated to me			
I forget things like homework, lunch supplies			
In the middle of something I forget what I am supposed to do.			
My mind tends to wander.			
You forget what you wanted to say when your hand has been up a while.			

For each check in sometimes or often complete the following

I need to do less of...   I need to do more of...

I learned that I'm good at

Name: _____   Date: _____

Executive Function Skills

Flexible Thinking & self control
Adapting when things change.

Check the boxes that are true for you	often	Sometimes	Rarely
I can agree to disagree nicely.			
I take time to learn from my mistakes.			
It is hard for me when things change.			
I can solve problems when they happen.			
Changes in the schedule make me nervous.			

For each check in sometimes or often complete the following

I need to do less of...	I need to do more of...

I learned that I'm good at

Executive Function Skills

Name: _____ Date: _____

Perseverance

Staying on task even when it gets tough

Check the boxes that are true for you.

	Often	Sometimes	Rarely
I tend to put things off until the last minute			
I'll finish it tomorrow if I don't feel like doing it.			
I have a hard time sticking to things.			
If I don't like it, it takes me long time to finish			
If it too hard, I give up			
I don't have patience for things that require a lot of effort.			
I'll avoid challenges rather than choose them			

For each check in sometimes or often complete the following:

I need to do less of...   I need to do more of...

I learned that i'm good at:

Executive Function Skills

Name: _____   Date: _____

Attention/Focus

Focusing on one task for a period of time

Check the boxes that are true for you	Often	Sometimes	Rearly
I get distracted and don't always want to start tasks.			
My work is often late.			
I tend to 'waste time' instead of doing the things i need to do.			
I mis-judge how a task might take me.			
I put things off and rush at the last minute.			

For each check in sometimes or often complete the following:

I need to do less of...   I need to do more of...

I learned that I'm good at

Name: _____   Date: _____

Self Reflection
Thinking about your learning & how you grow

Check the boxes that are true for you	often	Sometimes	Rarely
I finish thing quickly or rush through.			
I avoid solving problems.			
I need instructions Repeated to me.			
I need to think about how my actions effect others.			
I wait my turn patiently			
It is hard to read peoples Face & body language			
I am a capable student and I do my best			

For each check in sometimes or often complete the following

I need to do less of...	I need to do more of...

I learned that I'm good at

REFERENCES

Clark, A. (2022, March 31). *80% of Parenting is Modeling.* The Parent Practice. Retrieved 20 October 2022, from https://www.theparentpractice.com/blog/80-of-parenting-is-modelling

Laybourn, S., Frenzel, A. C., & Fenzl, T. (2019). Teacher Procrastination, Emotions, and Stress: A Qualitative Study. *Frontiers in psychology, 10,* 2325. https://doi.org/10.3389/fpsyg.2019.02325

The Research Institute for Learning and Development (n.d.). *A Fun Way to Talk About Shifting and Cognitive Flexibility.* Retrieved 20 October 2022, from https://smarts-ef.org/blog/fun-way-to-talk-about-shifting/

American Psychological Association. (2019, May 2). *Perseverance toward life goals can fend off depression, anxiety, panic disorders* [Press release]. https://www.apa.org/news/press/releases/2019/05/goals-perseverance

Louick, R. (n.d.). *Growth Mindset vs. Fixed Mindset: Key Differences and How to Shift Your Child's Mindset.* Big Life Journal. Retrieved 20 October 2022, from https://biglifejournal.com/blogs/blog/growth-mindset-vs-fixed-mindset-differences-and-how-to-shift-your-childs-mindset

Hall, P. A. (2022, January 1). *Executive dysfunction following SARS-CoV-2 infection: A cross-sectional examination in a population-representative sample.* medRxiv. Retrieved 20 October 2022, from https://www.medrxiv.org/content/10.1101/2022.01.01.22268614v4

Waterford.org. (2021, October 6). *Why Strong Teacher Relationships Lead to Student Engagement and a Better School Environment.* Retrieved 20 October 2022, from https://www.waterford.org/education/teacher-student-relationships/

Executive Functioning and Learning: 6 Ways to Help Your ... - Understood. https://qa.understood.org/en/articles/executive-functioning-issues-and-learning-6-ways-to-help-your-grade-schooler

"Children must be taught how to think, not what to think." Margaret .... https://teachdifferent.com/podcast/children-must-be-taught-how-to-think-not-what-to-think-teach-different-with-margaret-mead-education/

Growth Mindset Vs. Fixed Mindset | Big Life Journal. https://biglifejournal.com/blogs/blog/growth-mindset-vs-fixed-mindset-differences-and-how-to-shift-your-childs-mindset

Why Strong Teacher Relationships Lead to Student Engagement and a .... https://www.waterford.org/education/teacher-student-relationships/

English Grammar Rules 101 - انگلیش کلینیک. https://rafieienglishclinic.com/upload/blog/behtarin%20ketab%20hay%20baraye%20yadgiri%20/jacobs_melony_english_grammar_rules_101.pdf

Jean Piaget (1896-1980) Was A Cognitive Constructivist. https://www.bartleby.com/essay/Jean-Piaget-1896-1980-Was-A-Cognitive-P3E8NG398EHW

Counseling, Psychotherapy, and Psychological Assessment .... https://mycommunitybehavioralservices.com/

Neuroplasticity: Why It Matters - Life and Business Coaching. https://confidecoaching.com/neuroplasticity-why-it-matters/

What Is Visualization Meditation And What Are the Benefits?. https://www.betterhelp.com/advice/visualization/what-is-visualization-meditation-and-what-are-the-benefits/

How to develop a growth mindset in your organization. - Medium. https://medium.com/story-of-ams/how-to-develop-a-growth-mindset-in-your-organization-e28c4afeab69

6 Ways to Foster a Growth Mindset - Color of Your Thoughts. https://colorofyourthoughts.net/growth-mindset/

125 Brain Teasers for Kids (With Answers!)—Printable Brain Teasers for https://parade.com/1025662/marynliles/brain-teasers-for-kids/

10 teaching strategies to keep students engaged in the classroom. https://www.classcraft.com/blog/teaching-strategies-to-keep-students-engaged-in-the-classroom/

How to Measure a Goal (With Examples of Measurable Goals). https://www.lifehack.org/819321/measurable-goals

I have been telling everyone I know about the benefits of eating dried .... https://www.reddit.com/r/Jokes/comments/cjroul/i_have_been_telling_everyone_i_know_about_the/

It's Not That I'm So Smart, it's Just That I Stay with Problems Longer. http://

www.jeaninehughes.com/inspiration/its-not-that-im-so-smart-its-that-i-work-on-problems-longer/

Calvary Baptist Academy - New Braunfels, TX. https://cbatexas.org/

Made in United States
North Haven, CT
30 January 2024

48103312R10122